New
Library Service
TO Young Adults

Young Adult Library Services Association

WITH

Patrick Jones

EDITED BY

Linda Waddle

American Library Association
Chicago and London
2002

PATRICK JONES is the foremost national authority on young adult services in public libraries. He runs ConnectingYA.com, a firm dedicated to consulting, training, and coaching for providing powerful youth services. He is the author of *Connecting Young Adults and Libraries* and the recently published *Do It Right! Customer Service for Young Adults in School and Public Libraries*. He won the John Cotton Dana award in 1999 for a library card sign-up initiative and YALSA honors for ASPIRE, a homework center project. Jones holds an A.M.L.S. from the University of Michigan.

Composition in Janson Text and ITC Legacy Sans using QuarkXPress 4.1 for the PC

Printed on 50-pound white offset, a pH-neutral stock, and bound in 10-point cover stock by McNaughton & Gunn

The paper used in this publication meets the minimum requirements of American National Standard for Information Sciences—Permanence of Paper for Printed Library Materials, ANSI Z39.48-1992. ∞

ISBN 0-8389-0827-6

CONTENTS

ACKNOWLEDGMENTS

The road to the second edition of *New Directions* had many stops and many drivers. In particular, Carole Fiore, Elaine Meyers, and Renée Vaillancourt were involved in chairing or co-chairing the task force charged with the revision. Renée read all versions of the manuscript, provided great ideas, and helped shape the manuscript. Kudos also to the other members of the revisions task force: Kay Bishop, Sandra Payne, Jeff Blair, and Bessie Condos Tichauerr. Patrick Hogan from ALA Editions and Julie Walker from YALSA provided tons of assistance in helping shape the manuscript. But this is really as much Linda Waddle's work as mine. The former deputy director of YALSA, Linda consistently challenged me to make this work a bold step and statement about the role of libraries in youth development. *New Directions* isn't just a title change, it reflects Linda's belief on the road that libraries need to take when serving teens.

PATRICK JONES

Chapter 1

Directions

On September 11, 2001, students at Stuyvesant High School watched the destruction of the World Trade Center from their classroom windows. They saw the planes fly into the twin towers and, as the buildings collapsed, they saw flames shooting from the towers and watched in horror as people leaped to their deaths. After they were evacuated from their school, many of the students stayed in the area, instinctively wanting to help in any way they could. In the days following the attack, the students continued to volunteer to help in the rescue efforts. The football team served food to emergency workers; some students worked at supply stations or helped with fundraising efforts, while others painted murals of hope in Washington Square.

Peggy Sarlin, a Stuyvesant parent, wrote in the October 18, 2001, issue of *West Side Spirit*, "I have had the extraordinary privilege of observing their [Stuyvesant students] response to tragedy. I know many of us have worried about how good a job we've done as parents, raising this over-pressured, hyper-competitive, pop culture-obsessed, media-mad generation. But based on what I have seen, I am convinced our children are magnificent."

Although many teenagers have proven their worth in this latest tragedy, society remains ambivalent about them. Before September 11, young adults were also the focus of attention because of acts of violence in schools across the country.

Soon after the school shootings in April 1999 at Columbine High School in suburban Denver, Colorado, the three major weekly news magazines

(*Time, Newsweek,* and *U.S. News & World Report*) dedicated cover stories to explain to their readers why teenagers act the way they do. These stories looked at the physical, social, emotional, intellectual, and psychological development of teenagers. Similar stories appeared in other media and books were published that examine teens as a "tribe apart." The school shootings brought into the living rooms of many Americans a sense that something was terribly wrong with teenagers.

It is not the first time. A few years back, the media was focusing on youth violence in connection with gang activity. Since the "discovery" of juvenile delinquency in the 1950s coincided with rise of teen culture, teens have been easy targets for a nervous public. They are easily stereotyped and make good scapegoats. Many teens would disagree with the negative light under which their generation is portrayed on the nightly news and news-stands and seek to counter the perception among adults that something is terribly wrong with teenagers in the United States. They would argue that the problem is not with them, but rather how they are treated by adults. Clearly, there is a disconnect. This disconnection leads to alienation, stereo-typing, and the marginalization of teenagers so that they are perceived by adults as not having value. This message is reinforced not only by the media but also by institutions, such as libraries, where marginalizing teenagers is a standard way of doing business.

National youth policy has contributed to the marginalization of teenagers. Most programs have focused on only one problem, such as drug addiction or teen pregnancy. The times are changing, however, as during the 1990s a more holistic approach was introduced—the concept of positive youth development—that focuses on the needs and competencies of adolescents rather than on their specific problems. There has been increased interest in the "whole" adolescent and many adults and organizations are seeking ways to provide for their basic needs. Positive youth development focuses on the need for adolescents to have positive, ongoing relationships with adults and other young people and to be actively involved in their communities and a variety of activities that provide positive experiences in their free time. Simply stated, youth development focuses on building strengths as well as reducing weaknesses.

The holistic approach extends to the practices which best create healthy youth. It is not just the job of the school or the family, but rather the whole community. For when youth thrive, so does the community. Thus, every public institution, as well as private concerns, can and should play a role in building the strengths of young adults. That said, the fact is that only 11 percent of America's public libraries have young adult specialists on their staff to plan, develop, implement, and evaluate services to this important, influential, and growing user group (U.S. Dept. of Education 1995, 9). Given this vacuum, there is an increasing need to provide guidance and information to public librarians about understanding and meeting the unique needs of young adults. Young adults, as defined by the Young Adult Library Services Association (YALSA), are persons ages 12 to 18. In this publication, the terms *young adult*, *YA*, *teens*, *teenagers*, *adolescents*, *youth*, and *students* will all be used to describe this group of library users ages 12 to 18, who represent almost one quarter of the users of public libraries. It is estimated that by the year 2010 there will be more teenagers in the country than ever before (Aronson 2002). Clearly, public libraries will be looking at increased demands for their services by teenagers, but are the libraries ready for this age wave?

School library media specialists working in secondary schools face the same surge in the numbers of students. It is estimated that schools can expect 1.3 million additional high school students by 2009. School library media specialists face an almost Sisyphean task to integrate technology and information literacy into their programs, while under a great deal of pressure to maintain and expand other types of resources. The task would be difficult for even a seasoned school library media specialist, but projections indicate shortages of trained school library media specialists who are also certified teachers in the coming years. Both certified and noncertified staff members in the libraries of the nation's secondary schools will need guidance and information about library service to young adults.

This influx of teenagers in school and public libraries comes as libraries are still integrating an upsurge of information technology and electronic resources into their service responses. In this stormy climate of change, a clear direction is needed to guide services to young adults in school and public libraries. But at the same time, this climate of change demands looking toward the foundation of our services: what we value in serving teenagers and what value that teenagers receive from this service. Thus, this book looks at those values as directions, the traits in teenagers as assets, and the resulting connection of the two as outcomes. *New Directions* **isn't about how to better buy YA books or plan programs, but how through planning and viewing services to young adults in the larger youth development context, libraries can help youth thrive.**

BACKGROUND

The American Library Association's Young Adult Services Division first published *Directions for Library Service to Young Adults* in 1977. Young adult specialists, library school faculty, and administrators quickly and gratefully embraced it. This publication set a philosophical direction for service to young adults through examples from public library settings—examples that also had applications in other library settings.

The newly renamed Young Adult Library Services Association released the second edition of *Directions for Library Service to Young Adults* in 1993 to provide a framework for services to teens in schools and public libraries. The timing coincided with the association's publication, in conjunction with the Public Library Association, of *Bare Bones: Young Adult Services Tips for Public Library Generalists* by Mary K. Chelton and James M. Rosinia (YALSA/PLA 1993). *Bare Bones* filled in the framework; it provided the details and information for implementing the philosophy set forth in *Directions*, albeit only in the public library setting. *Directions* provided the "why" while *Bare Bones* delivered the "what," "where," and "how." In the introduction to the second edition of *Directions*, it was noted that "by fully supporting library service to young adults, the library community is much more likely to retain members of this age group as library users who will, as adults, become lifelong learners and library supporters." The work then spelled out in areas such as collections, programs, cooperation, information services, governance and administration, and access to information the major tenets of young adult library services, concluding with a reminder to libraries of their "responsibility to give equal consideration to the needs of young adults in planning and implementing library and information services."

Following a revised and expanded edition by Renée Vaillancourt of *Bare Bones*, renamed *Bare Bones Young Adult Services* (YALSA/PLA 2000), the concept of *New Directions* emerged. *Bare Bones Young Adult Services* is designed to train generalists *how to serve* teens; the goal of this document is to provide school library media specialists, young adult librarians, library administrators, and other interested parties with a structure to plan those services. *New Directions* provides the context for developing, implementing, and evaluating services to young adults. **Its purpose is to provide direction on how to establish quality library service to young adults in school and public libraries built upon the foundations of developmental needs, developmental assets, and youth development.** Developmental needs are tasks adolescents undertake as they grow from children to adults. Developmental assets refer to the positive factors that contribute to healthy youth development. Youth development is an approach toward youth that builds on their potential and helps counter the problems that may affect them.

The question is no longer merely asking what a young adult finds in a school or public library when entering it, but also what happens to that young adult as a result of checking out a book, participating in a book discussion group, spending time as a student assistant, or learning how to locate information on the Internet.

The focus is not only on the services libraries provide young adults, but also, just as importantly, on the outcomes of those services. Outcomes refer to the change in behavior brought about by a young adult using a library. By placing services in this broader context of developmental needs and assets and youth development, and by evaluating the outcomes of those services, administrators and other purse-string holders can begin to realize the true value of serving young adults in libraries. Librarians who serve young adults don't just develop collections; they help in the vital process of developing young people to become lifelong learners and competent, caring adults.

YALSA is not alone in taking this youth development approach. The federal government has funded several youth development studies, while local communities are embracing youth development through a variety of projects, most notably the Healthy Communities—Healthy Youth (HC-HY) initiative launched in 1996. Based on the Search Institute's framework of developmental assets, this initiative seeks to motivate and equip individuals, organizations, and their leaders to join together in nurturing competent, caring, and responsible adolescents. As of 2002, almost every state could report having an HC-HY community, which, in some states such as Colorado, have launched statewide initiatives. Two recent documents, *The Twenty-first Century Learner* by Beverly Sheppard (2001) prepared by the Institute of Museum and Library Services, and Samuel P. Whalen et al. (2001) *Connecting Young Adults to the Transforming Public Library*, issued by the Chapin Hall Center for Children, both place youth development square in the center as the motivation for, and the key to the success of, work with young adults. By taking the larger approach, by placing services to young adults in context of the bigger picture of youth development, elusive outcomes become apparent. **But just as important, the true mission of our work in libraries with teens becomes apparent to our profession, our community, and the teens we serve: our purpose is to help teens thrive and develop into caring, competent adults.**

PURPOSE

The specific goals of this work are to:

Provide guidelines on planning, implementing, and evaluating quality library service to young adults.

Use the developmental needs of adolescents, positive youth development, and the developmental assets as the framework.

Clearly state the core values of library service to young adults.

Utilize both the service responses (appendix A) presented in the *New Planning for Results* (Nelson 2001) and the goals in *Information Power: Building Partnerships for Learning* (AASL 1998) for a global point-of-view on service to young adults.

Provide success stories from libraries which have built services based on the core values.

Change the context for thinking about services to young adults in school and public libraries from a reactive series of programs aimed at increasing use of libraries, to a well-planned, proactive holistic service approach aimed at meeting developmental needs, developing assets, increasing student achievement, and creating positive outcomes.

This new edition of *Directions* (YALSA 1993) will incorporate ideas from the current planning documents of the American Association of School Librarians (AASL) and the Public Library Association (PLA). It will also integrate current trends from other organizations serving youth, in particular those focusing on youth development. While there are several different models in the growing field of youth development, the forty developmental assets model created by the Search Institute (appendix B) provides the best fit with library services, primarily because of its holistic approach to creating sustainable communities, which has been one of the recent focuses of the library profession. **The approach to library service for young adults also needs to be holistic and include families, teachers, and other members of the community who work to provide healthy youth development activities for young adults.** The context must be broader than the four walls and few ranges of shelving dedicated to young adult materials.

The landscape in which young adult services reside has changed dramatically since the last edition of *Directions*. There are changes in the context of daily life where teenagers are making their passage from childhood to becoming caring, competent adults. Much the same, changes in the context of the library setting are just as dramatic. These changes are extraordinary and affect every aspect of service. Rather than planning "film night" programs, young adult librarians are developing broad after-school programs which build assets in youth. The focus isn't just on after-school entertainment with a "one-shot" program, but rather with engaging teens daily with text and technology in such a way that they become more successful students and healthier human beings. Rather than just providing reference services to help students find information, librarians are planning ways to extend the use of technology to the underserved. Rather than looking only at young adult literature, librarians working with teens consider a wide variety of formats to deliver information, education, and recreation. Rather than merely selecting books which support school assignments, secondary school library media specialists are actively engaged in helping plan lessons and setting curriculum. Rather than printing book lists or pathfinders, librarians serving young adults, often with the involvement of young adults, are utilizing technology to provide improved access to their collections. Rather than focusing on numbers alone, young adult librarians are searching for impact, outcomes, improved grades and test scores, and positive youth development as the result of their work.

Finally, rather than providing services strictly *to* young adults, the youth development model, coupled with YALSA's commitment and support of meaningful youth participation, finds service delivery transformed into a collaborative context. Successful young adult services in school and public libraries emerge from the bottom up, not the top down. Young people are seen as assets to libraries, not just as customers. Services are planned *with* young adults, not merely for them. The needs of young adults come before the needs of librarians.

New Directions for Library Service to Young Adults looks away from what libraries have done for teens and looks ahead to the potential of what libraries can do *with* teens. The direction is away from hard standards related to number of volumes or types of specific programs to engaging in a whole service response which affects teens. Finally, the focus is not on the library, but on the community. **Libraries do not, should not, and cannot develop services for young adults because it is good for the library, but rather because these services will make an affirmative impact leading to positive outcomes for teens. Healthy youth create healthy communities in which libraries can thrive.**

Finally, this book will attempt to serve many purposes and reach different audiences in all types of libraries that serve young adults. This includes generalists, young adult specialists, school library media specialists, community college librarians and library school directors, college and university librarians, directors, board members, library trustees, principals, and superintendents. It will be used in graduate programs as well as for continuing education. State agencies, juvenile correctional facilities, and other youth-serving organizations will find it helpful. The YALSA Serving the Underserved trainers (see appendix C) who work with library generalists and other staff members in school and public libraries will use it as a basis for their training. It is both a statement of philosophy and a working document; throughout are excerpts from policy statements and checklists to use locally to provide direction for planning young adult library services. It is not a scorecard, a rubric, or a matrix; it is a checklist of ways that libraries respond to young adults through policies, collections, programs and services, technology, facilities and hours, and human resources.

Those responses are determined by linking the goals and the capacity of an individual library with the needs of young adults in the community. *New Directions* concludes with examples of librarians who have successfully made that link. There are eighteen examples of success stories from young adult librarians in school and public libraries who are making the "vision" real for the young adults in their lives. Several core documents are included in the appendixes, as well as bibliographies about young adult services, information literacy, and positive youth development. This work provides the direction to allow librarians to clearly state and demonstrate why services to young adults in school and public libraries must be moved from the margins and toward the center, where they and teenagers belong.

Chapter 2

Planning Your Trip

Imagine what your library's services to young adults could look like in the next five years. Could, would, or should it look something like this:

Every library in the community that serves young adults collaborates to develop a strategic plan to coordinate and provide the very best service to this age group. In every library, a librarian will be assigned the responsibility to provide service to young adults. Young adults will be working in the library in a variety of jobs. They will be volunteering during the summer and they will be working for the library on internships or as community service providers during the school year. Teens will still be using the library for homework and finding information that will result in increased achievement. In addition, they will find a broader selection of recreational materials, in particular music and magazines. There will be a large selection of customer-driven programs. Each secondary school and library will have a dedicated and appealing young adult space to use, as well as a range of outreach services, after-hours services, and web-based services which expand the library beyond its normal open hours. Teens will be savvy about using library technology to solve information problems and will have developed the skills to locate, use, and evaluate information from a wide variety of sources. All of these services will be planned, promoted, and implemented with the assistance of teens serving on formal or informal advisory groups, as well as with community partners. Finally, every young adult will view his or her library experience as a positive one and will not only return, but also promote, the library to peers. These positive interactions will contribute to the healthy development of young adults.

While there might be some differences if you were gazing out upon a school library setting, there are just as many similarities. What school and public libraries envision is similar: a context which nurtures positive youth development. That image, or vision, is the start of successful strategic planning. While it does not describe specific outcomes for users in detail, it is clear that the things we do in the library can really make an impact upon the lives of young people, especially when services are specifically planned to make that happen. While this vision could occur through happenstance, good luck, and the dynamic leadership of one person, any organization is likely to better reach its vision through the development of a strategic plan involving many stakeholders, including teens themselves.

This is, however, sadly not the case in most public or school libraries in relation to young adults. Long-range planning is normally limited to facilities and collections, not the services which emerge from those buildings. Annual plans are done in some, but not all (or enough) libraries that serve teenagers. To prepare this work, requests were made to school and public libraries for samples of long-range or strategic plans; few were received and those that were focused more on bricks and books than looking at larger services. Services come first: the bricks and the clicks and the books are the tools used to build those services. But too often, libraries allow resources to determine which services they will offer, rather than first asking the question about which services best meet the needs of young adult customers and then developing the appropriate resources to make those services occur and allow young adults to thrive in school and public libraries.

Of course, the best source of information about what young adults need is young adults themselves. They are the starting point for any planning that a library undertakes. Youth involvement is crucial to the planning process as it requires that adults recognize that young adults can make a positive contribution, and that adults respect the right of young adults to participate in decisions on matters that affect them.

There are many ways to involve youth in the planning process, from informal one-on-one conversations to formal focus groups put together with the help of a marketing research team. Surveys should certainly be utilized to gather information; teens may also be involved as volunteers in the distribution, collection, compilation, and analysis of the survey data. The surveys should allow an optional space for young adults to list their name, phone number, and e-mail address if they wish to provide more information. These young adults could then be interviewed through e-mail, or invited to a forum at the library to expand their ideas. Formal focus groups may be used or other methods for collecting information from teens and providing them with a chance to generate and share ideas. Organized teen groups which meet in public library meeting rooms or school libraries could be asked questions which inspire them to think of different directions for the library. School classes, such as those in service learning who are dedicated to working in the community, could provide input. Any or all of these methods send a clear message to young adults that their contribution is important. **Youth involvement in the planning process relates directly to the concepts espoused in youth development and developmental assets. When teens are involved it engages their talents, skills, and interests and demonstrates they are valued by the community and provides them with an opportunity to contribute to their community.**

The library and business literature is filled with tomes documenting the ins and outs of strategic planning; there is no need to rehash that here. It is necessary, however, to remind planners that there must be an alignment of a plan for service to young adults with the overall plan of the institution or group of institutions. The YALSA Strategic Plan is an example of planning at the national level that can serve as a model for other libraries planning library service to young adults (appendix D). Beginning with a vision that describes expected behaviors and outcomes of users, the planning process becomes a series of questions. *If* this is the vision we want to achieve, *then* what steps must be taken to reach that vision? The plan must first pose the questions, in many cases asking simple ones which tinker with the bottom line: Why have we always done it this way? *If* we want to achieve this vision, *then* what are the obstacles which stand in our way and how can they be overcome? If the obstacle is the resistance of other staff or administration, *then* what concrete to-do steps need to be taken to overcome those obstacles? In most cases, the obstacles relate to the capacity of the organization to meet certain goals. Capacity does not just mean resources ("we don't have enough staff"), but rather the organization's ability and ambition to achieve. Later, this work will examine two specific models for planning, one from the public library setting and the other from school libraries. Questions that create the environment for planning might include

What are the desired outcomes for the library?

What are the desired outcomes for young adult users?

What are the desired outcomes for the community?

What are the obstacles to reaching these outcomes?

What will increase the capacity of the organization to reach these outcomes?

What is the purpose of this plan?

How do services to young adults support the library's (or school's) overall strategic direction?

What is or has been the time line for developing and implementing this plan?

How will information be gathered from young adults, staff, members of the community, and interested partners?

What are the services required to meet the needs of the young adults in the school or community?

What will be the results of these short, near, and long-term services?

How will we measure the success of these services?

What issues need more study?

What are the next steps?

The process begins not by asking, "What do we need to do?", but by asking, "What is our vision of the library?" And beyond that, "What are the outcomes for young adults?" Strategic planning that involves other organizations in the community may result in a broader vision and would look something like this:

Young adults are privy to a wide range of experiences in diverse settings to develop adaptive skills and the confidence to use them. They thrive in a community that links families, governmental agencies, private and public organizations, and the faith community into a web of support. Youth participate in organizations, such as libraries, which see them as valuable contributors to their own development and assets to the community. Finally, all teens are nurtured as adults, and institutions realize that problem-free does not equal fully prepared, and dedicate resources toward inspiring positive youth development, not merely correcting problem behaviors.

Chapter 3 ————————————————————————

Maps

Could anyone in 1950 have envisioned library services to young adults as they exist at the start of the twenty-first century? In 1950, there was no Internet, no young adult literature, and very little teen-centered popular recorded music. While good people were doing good things with teenagers in schools and public libraries, there was not a shared special vision of what those services should look like.

So, how do we imagine services in the future?

It will be very different from what we know now.

And it will be very much the same.

It will be different because electronic resources, the great drivers of most library innovation and change efforts, will continue to develop. Technology will transform *how* libraries serve young adults. It will change dramatically *what* services and resources are offered. Just as public libraries discarded their album collections for racks of compact discs, those compact discs will soon be replaced by another format. It will certainly alter *when* and *where* teens will be served, just as the Internet explosion during the past few years has radically changed the location (anywhere) and timing (any-time) of some of the services offered to young adults. But even ten or fifty years in the future will not change *why* we serve young adults in libraries.

The reaction will be very much the same because services to young adults are based on the developmental needs of adolescents. Different groups present different frameworks, but first and foremost, the lives of young adults in the year 2050, like those in 2002 and 1950, will be still be centered around the same set of needs. The clothing will change, so will the context, but not the core needs of teens. These needs reflect the central drives in the lives of young adults: it is the stuff of their lives. According to American Academy of Child and Adolescent Psychology (1996), a teenager's life can be divided into three stages: early, middle, and late. The normal feelings and behaviors of adolescents for each stage are found in appendix E, "Normal Adolescent Development."

Understanding these needs does not involve a lesson in adolescent psychology; it is, instead, the foundation from which all planning of services for young adults in school and public libraries has, should, and will be built.

The issues facing libraries in serving teenagers at the start of the twenty-first century are centered around those needs. The push for information literacy, to ensure that every young adult understands not merely how to sit in front of a computer and type a search into Google, but also the process to access, evaluate, and use information, emerges from these needs. Young adult advisory groups, after-school programs, book discussion groups, booktalking in the schools, collections of popular magazines, chat rooms available via library computers, teen volunteers in school and public libraries, and the employment of young adults to work in libraries meet all of these needs. The books which teens read (or don't read), the programs they attend (or don't attend), the disruption they cause in the library through social interaction, and the value they bring to the library through volunteering address those needs. Every interaction with a teenager in a library is somehow influenced by that young person working through these needs and, thus, all planning of services begins by examining those needs. While teens develop at different paces, and often physical maturity and other development does not always go hand in hand, all young people are in motion. Teenagers are, like the unfinished construction project on the expressway, works in progress. How we respond to teenagers in the library helps determine how safely they make the passage from childhood to become competent, caring adults.

The planning process, thus, in any school or public library, becomes a meshing of the needs of young adults, the mission and goals of the organization, and the overall desires of the community. Expressed in a variety of ways, what most communities want is for teens to become caring, competent adults. They want their teens to be healthy, happy, and to avoid risky behaviors. They want them to do well in school, care about their neighborhood, and care about themselves. They want teens to succeed.

That is a vision that also has not changed radically since 1950 and probably won't change in the year 2050. The direction of services to young adults is not a straight line, but rather a circle where the intersection of the needs of the teens, schools and libraries, and the community at large meets. Those community services vary from large urban centers to small rural hamlets, from super-sized suburban high schools to small private high schools, and become part of the equation as well. The menu of services of a two-person public library in rural Michigan can differ greatly from the services emerging from TeenScape at the Los Angeles Public Library. The quantity of services is often determined by scale; the quality of services is determined by responsiveness to the needs of teenagers. A true vision of services to young adults in libraries isn't about young adult books, computers, or CDs; it is about making connections between what libraries offer and what young adults need. The new direction of services is to look at what young adults need first, and then to develop services to meet those needs. **The vision is about reconnecting with teenagers, forming relationships with them, and supporting them as they develop into adults.** As we look toward the future, a vision statement plays a vital role in planning for that future. In June 1994, the Board of the Young Adult Library Services Association adopted the following vision statement:

> In every library in the nation, quality library service to young adults is provided by a staff that understands and respects the unique informational, educational, and recreational needs of teenagers. Equal access to information, services and materials is recognized as a right not a privilege. Young adults are actively involved in the library decision-making process. The library staff collaborates and cooperates with other youth-serving agencies to provide a holistic community-wide network of activities and services that supports healthy youth development. (YALSA 2001, 1)

A vision statement represents many things to an organization; it is the reservoir from which missions, goals, and objectives flow. It tells everyone what the organization, representing its members working directly with young adults in school and public libraries across the nation, believes to be important. The vision responds to the needs of teens, not librarians. The vision provides the foundation on which goals are developed.

TWELVE GOALS

From such a vision statement, coupled with each library's or school's overarching vision and mission statement, a series of goals begin to emerge.

These goals represent what libraries do to make the vision of services to young adults a reality. While individual library goals should and will vary because of capacity and the overall goals of the library or school, the following goals represent the twelve building blocks of young adult success in school and public libraries:

Libraries:

1. Are committed to providing programs and services that are suitable to the developmental needs of young adults and the principles of positive youth development

2. Employ young adult specialists or certified school library media specialists, and train staff members, volunteers, youth participants, and others to serve young adults

3. Develop separate vision, mission, and goals statements for their programs

4. Provide for the unique needs of young adults as part of the library's general services, for example, readers' advisory, information services, cataloging, circulation, data collection, etc.

5. Set aside space(s) for young adults for their own use

6. Develop unique collections of resources for young adults

7. Provide equal access to buildings, resources, programs, and services for young adults

8. Treat young adults with respect and provide quality customer service

9. Utilize the experience and expertise of young adults

10. Provide remote information and resources needed by young adults for information, education, and recreation needs

11. Work together with other libraries in the community to build and strengthen the information literacy skills of young adults

12. Provide plentiful resources and enriching experiences to build and strengthen adolescent literacy skills.

In order to reach these goals, each library will need to develop specific objectives to plan, develop, and create the types of services that ensure these goals are reached. Later in this document, a checklist will be presented to provide guidance on specific objectives which might be undertaken to reach these various goals and fulfill the vision.

TEN CORE VALUES

The values upon which those goals, the vision statement, and this document are built provide the foundation for all services to teenagers in school and public libraries. All the "stuff" that librarians do are based upon ten core values:

1. **Developmental needs**
2. **Youth development**
3. **Developmental assets**
4. **Youth advocacy**
5. **Youth participation**
6. **Collaboration**
7. **Information literacy**
8. **Adolescent literacy**
9. **Learning and achievement**
10. **Equity of access and intellectual freedom**

If these values are in place when service to young adults is planned and implemented, successful outcomes are guaranteed. They are, not surprisingly, also the values which are elements of success in all youth programs because they focus on the positive, look beyond the four walls of an organization, and demonstrate youth advocacy in action.

1. Developmental Needs

Young adults use libraries in a variety of ways for a variety of reasons. Like any other group of customers, such as genealogists or businesspeople, their needs are unique. Not special, but unique. The needs (see appendix E) are directly related to where they are in their lives. One unique need of young adults, for example, is the need to socialize in groups. This is normal, but often problematic in a library setting. To respect the unique needs of teens is to respect this behavior and, as best as possible, to accommodate it. This push to be social emerges, as do most of the unique needs of young adults, from the various developmental milestones they encounter as they transform themselves from children into caring, competent adults. As these changes are occurring, behavior changes in all settings, including the library setting. **To respect the unique needs of young adults means to understand those needs, to accept them, to accommodate them, and to provide services which help to meet those needs.**

To respect those needs means that collections are responsive and reflect the diverse interests of young adults. It means that space is designed to accommodate teens, including a separate YA space. It means that electronic resources are plentiful, accessible, and that teen use of them is valued. But primarily, respecting the unique needs of teenagers means to not disrespect those needs. This emerges in all that we do, from collecting materials, such as professional wrestling or teen fashion magazines, which might conflict with our personal or community values, to the services we provide. **But mostly, respect is about the environment of the library and the attitudes of the staff. It is about culture.** For example, staff members in school and public libraries are concerned about teens "chatting" on their computers. Sometimes this manifests itself in blocking or filtering chat from computers, because of librarians' belief that chatting is a "waste" of time.

Yet nothing could be further from the truth. The value of chatting in teen life is huge: in addition to the fun and fad aspect which is rarely obvious to library staff, the social aspect of chatting makes a huge difference. To chat is to be able to express one's self, while at the same time holding back. To chat is to be able to explore and even experiment with self-image. Chat, Instant Messages, electronic mail, and other computer-assisted communication are becoming the dominant means by which teens relate to each other. **That gives it value. To respect the unique needs of young adults is to value what they value.** The value of chatting for many teens has the same value as that of the adult patron checking the stock market or the preschooler playing a CD-ROM. The value emerges not from the librarian's notions, but from the needs of the adolescent. **Teenagers are like the unfinished construction project on the expressway—works in progress.**

The primary method, however, through which librarians will or will not respect the unique needs of young adults is in the attitudes which underscore customer service. Librarians who respect the unique needs of teenagers will be approachable, nonjudgmental, and accepting. They will be encouraging, tolerant, patient, persistent, and emphatic. They will understand young adults, their psychology, their literature, and even their popular culture. They will understand the importance of providing opportunities for positive youth development. They will advocate for intellectual freedom, for free access, and for solving problems to knock down barriers to youth access. They will have a sense of humor, involve youth, and be creative. When they are like this, they are respectful. When young adults are given respect, they will respond in kind. By respecting the unique needs of young adults, libraries are creating a collaborative context, rather than an adversarial one. They are creating an environment which welcomes teens, rather than repels them. They are creating healthy youth, rather than becoming another member of the chorus which writes off teens as troublesome. **By respecting the unique needs of teenagers, libraries show that teens are not, in the words of YA advocate Ed Sullivan, "luggage to be handled," but rather customers to be served, readers to be engaged, and human beings to be developed (2001).**

2. Youth Development

According to the National Collaboration for Youth (NCY),

> **Youth development** is a process which prepares young people to meet the challenges of adolescence and adulthood through a coordinated, progressive series of activities and experiences which help them to become socially, emotionally, physically, and cognitively competent. Positive youth development addresses the broader developmental needs of youth, in contrast to deficit-based models which focus solely on youth problems. (www.nydic. org/nydic/devdef.html)

NCY also provides a definition for youth development programs:

> **Youth development programs** prepare young people to meet the challenges of adolescence and adulthood through a structured, progressive series of activities and experiences which help them obtain social, emotional, ethical, physical, and cognitive competencies. They address the broader developmental assets all children and youth need (such as caring relationships, safe places and activities, health and mental health, marketable skills, and opportunities for service and civic participation), in contrast to deficit-based approaches which focus solely on youth problems. (www.nydic.org/devdef.html)

A study conducted by the National Research Council and the Institute of Medicine (2001) identified eight features for successful youth development programs:

1. Structure and limits that are developmentally appropriate and that recognize adolescents' increasing social maturity and expertise
2. Physical and psychological safety and security
3. Opportunities to experience supportive relationships and to have good emotional and moral support

4. Opportunities to experience a sense of belonging

5. Opportunities to be exposed to positive morals, values, and positive social norms

6. Opportunities to be efficacious, to do things that make a real difference, and to play an active role in the organizations themselves

7. Opportunities for skill building, including learning how to form close, durable human relations with peers that support and reinforce healthy behaviors, as well as to acquire the skills necessary for school success and successful transition into adulthood

8. Strong links between families, schools, and broader community resources. Examples include leadership development, character enrichment activities, mentoring activities, community youth centers and clubs, community libraries, after school, weekend, and vacation programs, sports and recreation, book discussion groups, academic enrichment, environmental enrichment, preparation for work activities, community service, teen advisory groups, and civic participation.

Youth development is a perspective that emphasizes providing services and opportunities to support all young people in developing a sense of competence, usefulness, belonging, and power. While individual programs can provide youth development activities or services, the youth development approach works best when entire communities offer youth development opportunities. This can occur when a community as a whole agrees upon standards for what all young people need to grow into happy and healthy adults and then creates a continuum of care and opportunities to meet those needs. Youth development is also about strengthening families and communities and involving young people in those efforts. For that reason, youth serving agencies, including YALSA, have joined with the federal government to call for making youth development a national priority, as spelled out in the "Toward a Blueprint for Youth: Making Positive Youth Development a National Priority" statement (see appendix F).

Youth development is about prevention as opposed to intervention. Youth development has emerged as a vital and vibrant force in the youth field because of the change in perspective of seeing young people's journey to adulthood differently. Or, as Pittman and Fleming, two proponents of positive youth development, wrote:

For years, Americans have accepted the notion that—with the exception of education—services for youth, particularly publicly funded services, exist to address youth problems. We have assumed that positive youth development occurs naturally in the absence of youth problems. Such thinking has created an assortment of youth services focused on "fixing" adolescents engaged in risky behaviors or preventing other youth from "getting into trouble." Preventing high risk behaviors, however, is not the same as preparation for the future. Indeed, an adolescent who attends school, obeys laws, and avoids drugs, is not necessarily equipped to meet the difficult demands of adulthood. Problem-free does not mean fully prepared. There must be an equal commitment to helping young people understand life's challenges and responsibilities and to developing the necessary skills to succeed as adults. What is needed is a massive conceptual shift—from thinking that youth problems are merely the principal barrier to youth development to thinking that youth development serves as the most effective strategy for the prevention of youth problems. (1991)

The essential concept of positive youth development is that a successful transition to adulthood requires more than avoiding drugs, violence, or precocious sexual activity. The promotion of a young person's social, emotional, behavioral, and cognitive development is beginning to be seen as key to preventing problem behaviors themselves.

Clearly, these are objectives which libraries can help youth meet by responding with collections, technology, facilities, and programs. But, more importantly, services need to be created that foster these outcomes.

If school and public libraries are to remain vital, vibrant, and valued into the twenty-first century, it is essential that they refine and perhaps even redefine their role as key players in the process of supporting positive, healthy youth development. Librarians are paid by tax dollars by the public which expects many things. Most of all, the public expects libraries, like any other tax-supported institution, to make the community a better place to live. Librarians do that when they support youth development; when they help youth to develop healthily, by engaging youth in positive behaviors; when they empower youth so they thrive rather than engage in risk-taking behavior; and when they believe in youth so much that youth will believe in themselves rather than become stuck in a cycle of despair. When they do all of these things and so much more, they are supporting youth development. **Circulating books, answering reference questions, teaching information literacy, developing programs, forming youth advisory groups, promoting reading through booktalking, and every other positive action that libraries take support healthy youth development. These are not ends; they are means.**

3. Developmental Assets

Assets are factors promoting positive teenage development. These assets may result from "external" factors such as positive relationships in families, friendship groups, schools, and the community, or they may result from "internal" factors reflecting the teenager's personal convictions, values, and attitudes. Assets can equip adolescents to make wise choices. Some assets are encouragingly common among youth—caring about people's feelings and educational aspiration. Other assets are alarmingly rare—positive school climate, positive peer influence, and parent communication. (Benson, 1999)

Libraries don't serve youth because it is good for the library, but because it is good for young adults. What is good for young adults, it follows, is good for the community. That is the assumption. The Search Institute, a nonprofit organization whose mission is to advance the well-being of adolescents and children by generating knowledge and promoting its application, has transformed this idea into the vision that healthy communities are built through healthy youth. This vision is based on extensive research on youth which has produced a "developmental assets" framework. The forty development assets (Search Institute 1997) are the factors which are critical to a young person's successful growth and development (appendix B). These forty assets are positive experiences, opportunities, and personal qualities that all youth need in order to become responsible, successful, and caring adults. These are the critical factors for young people's growth and development. When gathered together, they offer a set of benchmarks for positive youth development.

The forty assets are divided into eight large groups:

- Support
- Empowerment
- Boundaries and expectations
- Constructive use of time
- Commitment to learning
- Positive values
- Social competencies
- Positive identity

These eight areas are the foundation young adults need in order to thrive.

The Search Institute, through research and application, concluded that **the more assets young people experience, the less likely they are to** engage in a wide range of risky behaviors and the more likely they are to engage in positive behaviors. Those positive behaviors include

- Succeeding in school
- Helping others
- Valuing diversity
- Maintaining good health
- Resisting danger
- Exhibiting leadership
- Delaying gratification
- Overcoming adversity

Sadly, the research also shows that many of young adults do not have assets. Research reported in the Search Institute's (1999) *A Fragile Foundation: The State of Developmental Assets among American Youth* shows that **only 38 percent of young adults reported having at least twenty of the forty assets** (16). One of the least reported of all the assets is reading for pleasure: less than a quarter of youth surveyed reported having this asset. While the assets framework is expanding, the research is currently based on young adults, students in grades six to twelve.

Relationships are the key to asset building. This is not social work; this is people work; this is library work with young adults. Forming relationships with teens, with teachers, other librarians, and others, helps pull youth away from the margins. Libraries at the center of their schools and communities are an equally strong selling point. Assets give libraries a way back to the center, which, given home computers, Internet cafés, super bookstores, and school computer labs, is of great value. At a time when many libraries are making decisions about services and programs, the use of the developmental assets approach can be helpful. But what libraries offer that none of those other places can offer is the possibility of quality customer service. What the library offers isn't so much bricks or cliques, but expertise. Libraries are not really in the information business or the book business, but the people business. **The essential role of any library serving any customer is about connecting people and information. Thus, it is about relationships.** This approach is not so much about adding new programs, services, after-school projects, teen volunteers, teen advisory councils, or even changing collections. **The key is putting the stuff that librarians working with young adults do every day into the asset framework: it is an easy fit.**

On the most basic level what young adults need and what libraries offer is an opportunity to develop relationships. Every reference question, every customer service interaction is an example of a fleeting (and in some cases, perhaps, not so fleeting) relationship. How a teen is treated in that moment, during that moment of truth, determines so much, means so much, yet is so easy. At the reference desk, the circulation desk, during an outreach activity, and especially in everyday life, libraries can build the assets by following the six principles of asset building:

- All youth need assets
- Everyone can build assets
- Asset building is an ongoing process
- Relationships are key
- Delivering a consistent message is crucial
- Duplication and repetition are necessary.

The slogan used by the American Library Association for years, Libraries Change Lives, could just as well have been Librarians Change Lives. Librarians change lives through the relationships they develop and the services they build based on those relationships. **Building assets, creating healthy youth, and strengthening communities are some vital roles for librarians serving young adults to plan for and to become participants in the twenty-first century.** Redefining the role of librarians helps to better plan services, helps to better explain to the public the outcomes of working with youth in libraries. But perhaps just as important an outcome is adopting the assets framework that allows librarians to measure the work they do, to see how the things they do actually improve the lives of young people by building the assets which will keep teenagers healthy, successful in school, and free from at-risk behaviors.

4. Youth Advocacy

Youth advocacy is almost deeper than a core value. **Youth advocacy is to services to young adults what water is to fish and oxygen is to humans.** It is the very core essence of what we do. Dorothy Broderick, the founder of *Voice of Youth Advocates* magazine, defined a youth advocate as "a person who believes in creating the conditions under which young people can make decisions about their own lives." Youth advocacy means believing that youth should be treated as "first class citizens" in the library world, not as poor cousins. Youth advocacy means believing that services for teens are a right, a given, and an indispensable part of the very business of every library, not an afterthought or a "special program." Youth advocacy means believing that every young person who walks through the door of a library deserves respect, attention, and our best efforts. Youth advocacy means being a voice with and for youth at all levels of a library organization, from ensuring that circulation systems can measure teen use to selecting appropriate furniture to providing information literacy instruction to programs which increase student learning and achievement. **Youth advocacy means believing in youth.**

Youth advocacy means believing in the best of youth, not accepting media stereotypes. It means engaging youth, rather than ignoring or judging them. Youth advocacy means providing youth with a voice, either directly through youth involvement or indirectly by standing up for the rights of youth. Youth advocacy means recognizing that adolescence is a time of passage and that the role of adults, especially those working in institutions like libraries, is to do everything possible to ensure the trip is successful. That belief is the foundation of our values, our attitudes, and our actions. Ultimately, youth advocacy means finding, celebrating, and sharing the value of young adults in libraries and in our communities.

5. Youth Participation

The term **"youth participation"** is probably unique to the library profession—it is certainly not a familiar term in youth development literature. YALSA defines the phrase as the "involvement of young adults in responsible action and significant decision-making which affects the design and delivery of library and information services for their peers and the community."

A better term might be "youth involvement." Whichever term is used, it is a broad concept that casts a wide net and is the cornerstone value of a new way of thinking about library services to young adults in the youth development movement. It involves any project, program, and practice which allows teens a chance to be more than customers. According to the National Collaboration for Youth (2001), "young people, as volunteers and partners with adults in decision-making, are a considerable—yet largely untapped—resource, representing a significant contribution to the social fabric of the nation."

Youth participation or involvement in libraries encompasses practices such as teen volunteer programs, teen book selection groups, and teen advisory groups. Youth involvement is about relationship building between librarians and teenagers through many different vehicles. While surveys, polls, and comment cards represent one type of youth involvement, simply asking teens, "What do you think about this?", is just as important. Youth involvement is an action, but mostly it is attitude. YALSA's Guidelines for Youth Participation are found in appendix G.

Youth involvement is respect in action. It builds on the idea that the voice of youth is important, it matters, and it should be allowed to be heard. Youth involvement allows teens to make a contribution to the library and thus to their community. Youth involvement benefits everyone involved: the library, which gains energy, ideas, enthusiasm, and extra sets of hands; the librarian, who gains value in watching young people learn and grow; the community, which finds youth actively involved and making a difference; and the young people themselves.

For a young adult, youth participation provides a wide variety of benefits. Regardless of the task at hand, youth involvement validates the importance of youth's contribution. Youth involvement can help young persons gain or develop a sense of responsibility, self-esteem, and meaningful participation. They gain skills, they gain knowledge, and they develop personal traits which will help them succeed. They develop a sense of being part of something larger: youth participation is citizen participation in action, making a difference at the local level. Youth involvement allows young people to interact with peers, as well as adult role models. It allows them to use their time constructively, to channel their energy into a positive project, and to contribute. For all these reasons, youth involvement is a cornerstone value of services to young adults because the outcomes directly meet the developmental needs of teenagers, while at the same time meeting the needs of librarians to provide the best services possible. It moves libraries beyond building collections or answering reference questions to making a real difference in the lives of young people by allowing them opportunities to build themselves.

The belief in youth participation leads to a strong belief in the value of using youth as volunteers and employees. Youth as a human resource is found in both public and school libraries. In either setting, youth can truly be empowered to take on areas of responsibility far above stamping date-due cards. Under proper guidance, youth can flourish in libraries: they can become fund-raisers, collection developers, merchandisers, and programmers, as well as fulfilling a host of other roles. In doing so, school library media specialists and librarians in other libraries who work with young adults are encouraging young people to go into the profession; helping them bond with libraries, books, and lifelong learning; and creating powerful youth advocates.

The value of youth participation is clearly not just in libraries, but in any organization serving youth. While there are various considerations, especially in unionized environments about the type of work which teens can engage in, the real issue is not about allowing youth to do so, but allowing adults to empower youth and teach them (Whalen et al. 2001).

6. Collaboration

Collaboration is a value that needs to be more extensively utilized by libraries. There is a strong correlation between quality library service and a higher success rate when libraries partner with other agencies. Collaboration and cooperation is attractive for many reasons, but there is now scientific evidence that it works. The proof that it works has been published in *Community Programs to Promote Youth Development*, from the National Research Council and the Institute of Medicine (2001). The report "gives an intellectual underpinning to conventional wisdom," says Ronald Ferguson, a Harvard professor and youth researcher (Boyle 2001, 38). The report concluded that young adults who are in communities with plentiful and varied developmental opportunities experience less risk and demonstrate higher rates of positive youth development. The more the variety and number of program offerings in a community, the more likely that the needs of a greater number of adolescents can be met.

Outside the world of libraries, collaboration is seen as one of the elements in success of developing youth programs. When libraries join such efforts, the safety net for teens grows larger. Collaboration is about sharing information, sharing resources, and sharing successes. **It is through collaboration and partnerships that individuals, agencies, and institutions with different methods, means, and motives can come together for the common goal of creating healthy youth.** "In partnership, museums, libraries and others can create a flexible learning ecosystem, a community campus of resources for all. They can address the learning divide that threatens our society and explore ways to provide the skills, resources, tools, and learning dispositions that all learners need." (Sheppard 2001, 9)

In the public library setting, collaboration with schools, youth-serving agencies, businesses, the faith community, government bodies, cultural institutions, and educational bodies that serve teens increases the strength of each group's program and tightens the safety net for teens in the community. Collaboration, in addition to the positive outcomes it can bring to young adults, provides the library with an opportunity to expand its base, state its message, and secure supporters in the community. Collaboration is often one of the keys to grant funding, to improved visibility of the library and youth issues in the community, and another method by which the public library integrates itself into the larger human services network. It is where we can share what we bring to the table in promoting positive youth development.

The most natural collaboration for public libraries, and almost always the most successful, are relationships with schools. Strengthening the bonds between schools and public libraries benefits everyone. One of the keys to providing quality young adult services in the public library is to develop a quality working relationship with schools. For schools, the advantages to working with the public library are numerous. Cooperation can complement a school's own educational resources, promote sharing of resources in a time of diminishing budgets, help in developing innovative programs and activities, broaden students' access to information and materials, and enhance a student's information literacy. For public libraries, all of these advantages hold true and, in addition, public libraries benefit greatly from working with schools as it allows them to provide better service to students by having more information about their needs, to promote programs and services to the "captive audiences" which schools can provide, to fulfill their educational mission, to strengthen bonds with the community and, most importantly, to eliminate misunderstandings and frustration of students.

Again, collaboration is only a means to an end. The desired outcome is to have students using all types of libraries with a high degree of satisfaction and success and a low amount of frustration and failure. In addition, the outcomes of improved collaboration for students include increased access to information, the ability to obtain materials easily, a library staff with a better understanding of student needs, reduced stress and time spent using libraries, increased access to recreational reading, increased access to information technology, and a higher level of information literacy.

7. Information Literacy

Information literacy is the ability to access, evaluate, and use information from a variety of sources. By providing youth with instruction on how to become information literate, librarians and others are providing young people with a survival skill. If young people are to not only survive but also thrive in the twenty-first century they must have the skills to find, evaluate, and use information; a skill they will need if they are to become lifelong learners.

An information literate person is one who

Recognizes the need for information

Recognizes that accurate and complete information is the basis for intelligent decision-making

Formulates questions based on information needs

Identifies potential sources of information

Develops successful search strategies

Accesses sources of information including computer-based and other technologies

Evaluates information

Organizes information for practical application

Integrates new information into an existing body of knowledge

Uses information in critical thinking and problem solving. (Doyle 1992, 2)

The outcomes for working together in the arena of information literacy are adults who become lifelong learners and members of an information literate society.

Collaboration between school library media specialists and teachers is the beginning, not the end, of successful information literacy instruction. It is time to formally acknowledge that "the responsibility for learning is not the exclusive preserve of formal educational institutions and training centers; it is a community-wide responsibility." (Sheppard 2001, 5)

Learning information skills begins when school library media specialists work with teachers and curriculum departments. They work together to plan for instruction supportive of curriculum integration, and to design, then implement, a variety of strategies and experiences that engage each student in successful learning.

Through collaboration, school library media specialists can ensure that information literacy is not merely a part of the curriculum, but instead is integrated like other basic skills into every classroom. Collaboration with other learning institutions leads to the extension of Information Literacy Standards for Student Learning in *Information Power: Building Partnerships for Learning* (AASL 1998; see appendix H). The goal of the information literacy standards is to ensure that young adults leave high school able to participate fully in a learning community, where everyone, not just students, is "interconnected in a lifelong quest to understand and meet our constantly changing information needs."

The result is improved student learning and positive youth development. Students are engaging in reading, writing, speaking, viewing, and listening for enjoyment, enrichment, and understanding. By placing a value on collaboration, libraries as well as young adults will reap tremendous benefits. Any organization that seeks the same outcomes as libraries, from museums to youth-serving agencies, should be considered as possible partners to support information literacy.

8. Adolescent Literacy

Although the literacy movement in the United States is strong, the literacy needs of young adults do not receive much attention. While everyone recognizes how important it is for children to learn to read by grade three, there is a tendency to forget that reading development is a continuum, and the result is that emphasis on literacy decreases after elementary school.

When administrators in school and public libraries question the allocation of resources to address **adolescent literacy** needs, librarians who work with young adults will find a growing body of knowledge to support print literacy as well as information literacy in their programs:

> Internationally, the United States scored in the middle on a new 32-nation study of educational achievement conducted by the Organization for Economic Cooperation and Development. The United States has many of the best readers in the world—and a larger number of the worst readers. While 10 percent of the U.S. 15-year-olds taking the exam scored in the top ten, 18 percent scored at or below the lowest performance level, which means they were unable to identify themes of reading assignments or locate basic information within a text. This is the same percentage as the international average, but more than twice as high as Finland and Canada, the countries that scored the highest in reading. The results about reading from a survey of 15-year-olds' achievement indicate that "most U.S. students leave the primary grades as competent readers steeped in the basics, but many fail to refine and build on their skills as they move through middle and high school." (Hoff 2001, 7)

There is a difference in the attention given to literacy skills between the highest performing and the lowest performing students in America's schools. Research indicates that low-performing students are twice as likely as high-performing students to be enrolled in less difficult and challenging language arts classes. Because they read and write poorly, they are required to read and write less. An assessment conducted by the Southern Regional Education Board tested more than 50,000 "career-oriented" students and found that only 11 percent, barely one-tenth of the career-oriented seniors, read well enough to continue their education and advance in the world of the future, where they must process and understand new and often complex information. "The poor reading skills of these high school seniors is not a problem of genetics or ability. Rather, schools are failing to engage many students in completing challenging reading and writing assignments. In addition, state and local school boards do not demand that schools make 'literacy for everyone' a top priority and do not provide the needed financial and program support." (Bottoms 2001)

The latest reading test scores from the National Assessment for Educational Progress (NAEP) indicate reading scores have made no significant statistical gains since the 1970s. They also report that a smaller percentage of 13- and 17-year-olds read for fun during 1999 than in 1971. In addition, the number of different types of reading materials available in homes has decreased, and a smaller percentage of 17-year-olds saw adults reading in their homes during the same time period. (NAEP 1999)

Along with "Adolescent Literacy: A Position Statement" from the International Reading Association (appendix I) that is discussed below, librarians working with young adults can make a powerful argument for using their resources to encourage reading and assisting all teen readers to hone their reading skills.

"Adolescent Literacy: A Position Statement" calls attention to the need for guidance in the more advanced stages of literacy. It consists of a set of principles to support adolescent literacy growth. The first and foremost is: "Adolescents deserve access to a wide variety of reading materials that they can and want to read." In support of this principle, it proposes that literacy research and professional judgment support at least four reasons for providing adolescents access to inside- and outside-of-school reading materials they can and want to read:

Time spent reading is related to reading success

Time spent reading is associated with attitudes toward additional reading

Time spent reading is tied to knowledge of the world

Reading is a worthwhile life experience.

According to the statement on adolescent literacy, positive outcomes can only be accomplished "through a network of educators, librarians, parents, community members, peers, policy makers, technology providers, and publishers," who shape the following elements:

Time—Adolescents deserve specific opportunities to schedule reading into their days.

Choice—Choosing their own reading materials is important to adolescents who are seeking independence.

Support—Time and choice mean little if there is no support. Support includes actions such as bringing books to the classroom, arousing interest in them, orally reading selections, and fostering student-to-student and student-to-adult conversations about what is read (Commission on Adolescent Literacy 1999).

A young adult's ability to use most of the resources available in school and public libraries depends upon the ability to read. While it is not the role of a library to teach reading, the issue of adolescent literacy is one which anyone working with teens needs to have on their radar screens. The statement on adolescent literacy outlines active steps, which anyone who is concerned with the issue can take.

Support for adolescent literacy begins with an understanding of some of the reasons why young adults choose not to read. Teens who are poor readers will certainly associate reading with failure. Developing collections which contain high interest but low vocabulary materials may increase the chances that teens will succeed. Audio books, comic books, and even a collection of high-teen-appeal children's books may help struggling young adult readers succeed. But even those with skills may be aliterate—they can read, but choose not to. Collection development, in those cases, might need to steer more toward nonfiction or magazines, which often does not require the same amount of time or concentration as fiction. Even teens that like to read often are confronted with negative pressures not to read, in particular, boys. Again, collection development in "hot" nonfiction areas and magazines works against this stigma. Decorating the library with something as simple as ALA Read posters, such as those featuring male sports or movie stars, may put reading in a more positive light. Many young adults do not receive encouragement to read at home, and therefore libraries and classroom teachers must positively reinforce reading.

This is a tricky proposition, however, as one reason many teens "reject" reading is because teachers or other adults force it upon them. It is only by establishing relationships, and thus breaking down this natural teen barrier, that librarians can begin to really encourage reading. Encouragement of reading can be programmatic with incentive-based programs, such as summer reading games, or it can be done across the reference or circulation desk with positive reinforcement messages. It can be as skilled as a detailed readers' advisory interview or as simple as a word of encouragement across the check-out desk.

The working stereotype is that teens don't read, that all they do is listen to music, play video games, and watch television. While reading is not the most popular recreational activity of teens, it still plays an important role. According to the survey conducted by YALSA and SmartGirl.org during Teen Read Week 2001, teens said they would read more if they had more time. That is good news for libraries: it shows the interest is there among young adults. And, in a demonstration of more than interest, the very optimistic results of the National Education Association's survey of teen reading found that young people recognize and identify reading as the most critical skill that they must master in order to be successful in life. Far from being anti-reading, **the research suggests teens see the value of reading in their lives.** If teens really do value reading, then libraries need to continue to nurture that response by promoting reading; even in the digital age, it is an important priority.

The National Education Association survey (NEA 2001) also found that teens both enjoy reading and are comfortable with and confident in their reading abilities. While there are teens who struggle, the majority of teens report that reading is not a source of failure for them. For many, reading is a huge source of enjoyment. The NEA research found that 42 percent of teens read primarily for "fun and pleasure," while 35 percent read for "facts and information." This is in contrast to Search Institute's research finding that only 25 percent of teens read for pleasure. Not surprisingly, like most things in teen lives, many teens are very passionate about their reading. The NEA found that 41 percent of teens read more than fifteen books a year.

The NEA survey, as well as the one conducted at SmartGirl.org, found that girls consistently express greater interest in and commitment to reading than do boys. Libraries need to look for ways to engage boys and encourage them to read. Boys' book discussion groups, a heavier emphasis on nonfiction and magazines, and allowing for boys' voices to be heard in youth involvement are all starters. Many teens surveyed indicated that libraries are part of the problem by not providing sufficient interesting reading material for teenagers. Despite the massive expenditures for electronic resources, librarians serving teens must continue to develop print collections which make teenagers want to take the time to read.

Teen readers fall primarily into four camps: the avid reader, the casual reader, the reluctant reader, and the nonreader. Each of these groups presents libraries with a unique set of challenges, but each group has some common needs. First and foremost is access to materials. In school and public libraries, this means a space where materials of interest to young adult readers are shelved, displayed, and featured. That might mean a young adult area or space, but it could also mean displaying young adult materials next to the Internet access computers or providing teachers with classroom collections. Access means every young adult needs to have a library card. A library card campaign can be a small but significant project, which not only serves teens, but also fosters collaboration between schools and public libraries. One of the keys to successful library card campaigns is to first look at policies and procedures which hinder youth from signing up for cards. In schools, policies and procedures on how and where students spend their time can serve as either a barrier to access or as an incentive for increased reading.

Many teen readers need a way to respond to what they have read. They need a chance to talk about the ideas in the books or the characters. As they respond, they deepen their appreciation for reading because the value of it becomes clear to them. Whether it be through programs or technology, libraries working with young adults need to provide teens with an opportunity or vehicle respond to books. Simply asking teens what they are reading and why they liked a particular book are powerful questions to building relationships with readers.

Young adult readers are all over the map. Some enjoy reading picture books, while others are willing to tackle James Joyce as a spring break project. Some read a book a night, while others read only when forced, and sometimes not even then. **But what all teen readers have in common is they are developing a relationship with reading. The essential role of the librarian serving young adults is to nurture that relationship.**

We learn about teen reading and contribute to improving adolescent literacy when we show respect for the reading choices of young people. We compliment; we don't condemn. If a young adult is reading comic books, we provide access to comic books and graphic novels. To say or to convey the attitude of "at least they are reading something" is to show disrespect for what the teen, for whatever reason, has chosen to read.

We learn about teen reading and contribute to improving adolescent literacy when we provide access to a wide range of materials for them to choose from and ensure that policies do not deny them access. For many teens, libraries are their only access to reading materials. We learn about teen reading and contribute to improving adolescent literacy when we talk to teens about their reading interests and tastes. In doing so, not only do we make our collections more responsive, but we empower teens by showing them their opinions have weight. Through book discussion groups, book review message boards, or reviews linked to the library's web page, to creating a reading interest survey to talking with teens about their reading histories, we not only involve teens, but we also actively engage them. We learn about teen reading and contribute to improving adolescent literacy when there is collaboration between schools and libraries.

Working with parents as well as with reading or English teachers, coaches, and other individuals interested in positive youth development will strengthen and nurture adolescent literacy. Collaboration with youth-serving agencies, with interested businesses which provide sponsorships and incentives, and with parent groups creates the bonds to form a strong reading community for young adults in schools and public libraries. A research study by Susan B. Neuman and Donna Celano (2001) studied the access to print in low-income and middle-income communities. They found that the role of the community in nurturing literacy is vitally important, but often overlooked. The study surveyed reading materials, signage, public spaces for reading, books in child-care centers, school libraries, and public libraries. They found that limited access to print resources meant the children did not gain familiarity and practice with exposure to print, thus creating a negative relationship toward initial and developing literacy. The lack of exposure and experiences with print led to less involvement in reading-related activities and less motivation to read. Although each of the communities had some print resources available to children, print resources for young adults were virtually nonexistent. In conclusion, Neuman and Celano stated, "Clearly, we need to strengthen these connections and build upon community assets if literacy is to be a cultural, social, and cognitive achievement for all children." (25)

Finally, when we do all of these things, we increase the chances that teens will become proficient readers. When they become readers, their chances to succeed in school increase. But just as important, reading for pleasure is a key asset that shows a young adult's commitment to learning. **The relationships we build with young adults to help them commit to learning demonstrate not just our values in action, but also demonstrate the value we see in young people.**

9. Learning and Achievement

One outcome of positive youth development is success in school. Increasing student **learning** and **achievement** is an important goal of public libraries and an essential one for the junior high or high school library. Student learning encompasses the broad process of learning, whereas student achievement is closely linked with success on standardized tests. Within the educational community there is debate as to which of these is more important, but to most students both are important. Few students enjoy failing any test, and most students, despite numerous obstacles, do want to learn. As schools focus on student learning and achievement, libraries serving teens must look at the role they can play. In school libraries, the value of a strong program is well documented in the variety of studies.

With growing research from states such as Alaska, Colorado, Texas, and Pennsylvania and similar studies happening in other states, the ability of school libraries to "back up" these words with facts is developing. In the Colorado studies, researcher Keith Curry Lance (2001) concludes that

> These findings provide evidence needed to answer three major questions about the impact of school library media centers on academic achievement.
>
> 1. Is there a relationship between expenditures for library media centers and test performance, particularly when social and economic differences across communities and schools are controlled?
>
>   *Yes.* Students at schools with better-funded library media centers tend to achieve higher average reading scores, whether their schools and communities are rich or poor and whether adults in their community are well or poorly educated.
>
> 2. Given a relationship between library media center expenditures and test performance, what intervening characteristics of library media programs help to explain this relationship?

The size of the library media center's total staff and the size and variety of its collection are important characteristics of library media programs that intervene between library media center expenditures and test performance. Funding is important precisely because its specific purpose is to ensure both adequate levels of staffing in relation to the school's enrollment and a local collection that offers students a large number of materials in a variety of formats.

3. Does the performance of an instructional role by library media specialists help to predict test performance?

   Yes. **Students whose library media specialists played such a role tended to achieve higher average test scores.**

Public libraries are expected to play a role here as well. Gallup polls have indicated that formal education support is seen by the public as an important role for public libraries to play, the assumption being that one purpose of this role is to support student learning and achievement. (Rodger 1994) There has yet to develop a body of research on the impact that public libraries have on student learning and achievement, even though public libraries are increasingly developing services based on this core value. Until the power of technology changed the way public libraries saw their role in education, training and instruction were seen as the sole province of the schools, and within the schools as a part of the school library media program. The need for constant training and instruction about new information technology has forced public libraries to take another look at their role in supporting student learning and achievement. If public library staff receives the proper instruction and training, then they can become full participants in the education of their customers. Communities no longer see formal educational institutions as the sole providers of learning, in part because of the recognition of the need for lifelong learning. Lifelong learning, the hallmark of any public library, begins by complementing the formal educational system through informal settings.

10. Equity of Access and Intellectual Freedom

The unique nature of young adults, no longer children yet not adults, is the central contradiction which emerges in the debate over **equal access to information.** When is a person considered an adult? The debate rages, in particular in the juvenile justice system. It depends on what state that person lives in, the political climate of the legislature, and what the young person wants to do or is to be punished for doing. Sixteen-year-olds can drive in most states. They are given the legal authority to operate a dangerous piece of machinery, yet that same person, in many libraries, might be still considered a child and be denied access to the Internet, video tapes, and other resources or services. The interest of the state in "protecting" people not yet considered adults bounces hard up against the well-established, although often challenged, position of the American Library Association of providing equal access regardless of age. In 2001, the American Library Association mounted a campaign to repeal the Child Internet Protection Act (CIPA), which primarily mandates that libraries receive e-rate discounts if they provide filtered Internet access to minors. Few things are as blatantly anti-equal access as the CIPA.

The debate, which has intensified to national proportions complete with court cases and media coverage, is nothing new. The dilemma associated with the urge to protect young people from certain types of materials has long been present in libraries. Many an adult can tell the story of being denied access as a child to the adult part of the library, or not being allowed to check out certain books. While the format has changed, the debate rages on. It is about teens having the same access to information as adults. Is some of the material that teens would access harmful? Of course, it is. But is it more harmful to deny access to information they want and need? Again, of course it is.

The importance of youth advocacy is especially evident when the library, through its policies and procedures, provides equal access to resources. Access begins in selection; libraries must purchase and promote materials that teenagers require to satisfy their varied needs. In particular, information about sexuality is not only of interest to teenagers for obvious reasons related to physical development, but also is necessary, even life-saving, information. Barriers to information on sexuality are numerous. An example of this was a very public challenge by radio talk show host "Dr. Laura" to YALSA's *TeenHoopla* (http://www.ala.org/teenhoopla) website that selected *Ask Alice*, a health information service from Columbia University, as a link from the website. The controversy here, although about a website rather than a book, was based on the same clash of principles: the desire by some to withhold information from teenagers about sexuality and the competing urge by youth advocates to provide teenagers with vital health information. **Rather than protecting young adults from information, which is something few teens would want or need, librarians must offer the resources and guidance to help adolescents make the transition to**

adulthood from resources selected especially for them in a variety of formats, including providing links to selected Internet sites and providing equal access to the Internet.

Acquisition of many library resources raises the question of whether approval or rejection of a given item is the result of selective judgment and discrimination or simply preselection censorship. This comes into play most often with materials which tend to challenge or question conventional ways of thinking and traditional values. But this questioning is a normal, natural, and necessary part of a young adult's right of passage. Resources must be selected for positive qualities, rather than excluded because they push the envelope. This has long been an issue in popular music collections, and it did not start with the rap music. The questions about collecting raw and raunchy rhymes of many current rap artists are the same as those posed to librarians about collecting popular music since the time of Elvis. Much the same, the current trend toward "gritty" young adult literature, which has received coverage in national news sources such as *Time* and the *Washington Post*, poses a similar question about what is appropriate reading material for young adults. Youth advocates and proponents of equal access realize that adults must allow teens to make their own choices from the wide variety of information and entertainment available to them. Equal access gives teens the opportunity to do this.

Equal access is not only about legal or policy barriers to youth access to information, but also about economic obstacles. If the key to improving adolescent literacy is ample access to reading materials, then the key to improving information literacy is ample access to sources of information, in particular those available via the Internet. A gap exists between those who can effectively access and use new information and communication tools, such as the Internet, and those who cannot. It is clear that there is a need to extend the use of electronic resources to the underserved in our society. While a consensus does not exist on the extent of the gap (and whether the gap is growing or narrowing), researchers are nearly unanimous in acknowledging that everyone in our society does not enjoy equal access to electronic resources at this point in time.

The main United States federal agency working on the issue of extending technology to the underserved has been the Department of Commerce's National Telecommunications and Information Administration. This agency has collected most of the research, issued press releases, and prepared the seminal report *Falling through the Net: Toward Digital Inclusion* (2000). The guiding principle of this work is that

In just about every country, a certain percentage of people has the best information technology that society has to offer. These people have the most powerful computers, the best telephone service and fastest Internet service, as well as a wealth of content and training relevant to their lives. There is another group of people. They are the people who for one reason or another don't have access to the newest or best computers, the most reliable telephone service or the fastest or most convenient Internet services. The difference between these two groups of people is what we call the "digital bridge." To be on the less fortunate side of the bridge means that there is less opportunity to take part in our new information-based economy, in which many more jobs will be related to computers. It also means that there is less opportunity to take part in the education, training, shopping, entertainment and communications opportunities that are available on line. Now that a large number of Americans regularly use the Internet to conduct daily activities, people who lack access to those tools are at a growing disadvantage. Therefore, raising the level of digital inclusion by increasing the number of Americans using the technology tools of the digital age is a vitally important national goal. (34)

Falling through the Net: Toward Digital Inclusion concludes that more than half of all households have computers and that more than half of all Americans will be using the Internet by the middle of 2001. Nevertheless, a gap remains or has expanded slightly in some cases, even while Internet access and computer ownership are rising rapidly for almost all groups. For example, data gathered for the report show that large gaps remain for blacks and Hispanics when measured against the national average Internet penetration rate (blacks 23.5% penetration rate; Hispanics 23.6%; compared with 41.5% of the total).

The Web-Based Education Commission's report, *The Power of the Internet for Learning: Moving from Promise to Practice* (2000), outlines a national agenda for addressing the issue of equal access to electronic resources. It is asking institutions from the federal government to the local school to engage in programs which narrow the gap between information haves and have-nots. The report calls for a national mobilization: "one that evokes a response similar in scope to other great American opportunities—or crises: Sputnik and the race to the moon; bringing electricity and phone service to all corners of the nation; finding a cure for polio." (11) The challenges of the equal access to electronic resources provide librarians working with youth with a myriad of opportunities for networking in the community, expanding resources through private and public funds dedicated to this project, and energizing communities in pursuit of this goal. The lack of equal access to electronic resources is not a "library" problem, but rather a real threat to communities where youth are disenfranchised from entry into the Information Age, as well as a barrier to positive youth development.

TEN ESSENTIAL ARGUMENTS

But are these values shared by public library administrators and school principals? Service to young adults, in particular in public libraries, is often viewed as a luxury or an extra, rather than essential. In school libraries, the building blocks of youth development and the support information literacy are often lost in the daily demands of providing services and in the shifting priorities of administrators. Every public and school library has resources to support young adult services; often, those resources are, however, allocated elsewhere. The issue is simply one of priorities. **To make increased services to young adults as a priority, youth advocates must be prepared to explain why serving young adults is an indispensable role.** Youth advocates, then, must be prepared to answer the following question: "Why library service to young adults?"

1. Young adult services are built on the needs of teens, but in order to be successful, the services must have support of the purse-string holders. The needs of the person or persons making resource allocations must be taken into account. Always, such an investigation must begin with determining the values of the library or school administration and connecting those with the values of young adult services. These values can normally be found in the mission statement of the institution. The values are carried out in how resources are allocated, by what programs or services are pushed to forefront, by how staff is allocated, and finally by what "clicks" with school boards and principals and with library boards and directors. Circulation of materials, student learning and achievement, visibility in the community, awards and honors, support for government officials, and creating a healthy community are a few of the "clicks" with school and library administrators. Young adult services can contribute to each of these administrative goals, and in doing so fulfill the goals of young adult services. **Thus, an essential argument for providing quality services to young adults in school and public libraries is that, in doing so, the larger organization can meet**

its goals, carry out its mission, and meet the public expectations of creating a better community.

2. Not only do **demographics** suggest that young adults are a growing population group, but research also supports the idea that the young adult age range is actually expanding. Puberty is occurring earlier and earlier; thus the passage of adolescence is beginning earlier. Given the influence of media and popular culture, the interest in things "teenage"—including books, magazines, and other materials which libraries provide—will start showing up earlier in children. Traditional children's services in public libraries are less important in the lives of children beginning perhaps as early as fourth grade; these children are interested in the culture of teenagers. And, of course, by adding the Internet to our libraries, more teens are pouring in, teens who may not have been users of traditional library services.

3. Teens use libraries; they use them a lot and they use them in a holistic fashion. For research, they may use sources ranging from a children's book to a reference volume, from a microfilm of an old newspaper to accessing the most current information available via the Internet. Doing well in school is an important goal for young adults, and many of them learn that libraries are the place that can help them. While teens make up almost one-fourth of public library users, no public library dedicates a quarter of its resources to serving young adults. (U.S. Dept. of Education 1995, 2) That makes sense, since a teenager's use of the library is not limited to those things which are shelved in a young adult area. But a commitment to serving young adults by a public library means providing the resources, including staff, to meet the needs of teens. A young adult librarian can improve the quality of the services offered by training other staff in the unique needs of young adults and draw more teens into the library by developing suitable programs and services. Teens are here; the best way to serve them is to develop a proactive strategic plan which is based on adolescent needs, youth development, and developmental assets. **Be proactive rather than reactive.** Less time and resources are wasted, collections are more likely to be circulated, programs more likely to be attended, and customers more likely to be served. Thus, young adult services are an efficient, and even cost-effective method for public libraries to best serve this large user group.

4. The demographics, but more importantly the headlines on the nightly news, support the idea that teens are in danger, in crisis. If that is the case, then as public institutions, libraries and schools are rightly expected to do the things which can help alleviate this crisis. **Libraries are part of the**

solution, but may also be part of the problem. We are part of the problem if our response to the changing context of teen lives is business as usual. The things we do to help teens bond with schools and libraries helps them bond with reading and books and information. Libraries provide a place for teens to form relationships which will help keep them from at-risk behavior. By supporting student learning and achievement, libraries can help students improve their grades and stay in school. Libraries can be a safe haven for teens and also a place to build teen community. If the headlines of the past few years have shown us anything, it is the danger for teens who don't feel connected to anything, who feel isolated and alone. Libraries, through programs and services, through youth involvement and youth outreach, provide opportunities to teens. Libraries are hangouts for teens, and that is a good thing. Like any group, their behavior needs to be managed and appropriate, but it is vital that teens feel welcome to be in the library and to talk with friends. The outcome of creating community in the library benefits everyone.

5. The perception of crisis among teenagers leads to a more practical reason for serving teenagers in schools and public libraries in terms of the financial benefits it can bring. **Serving young adults is how libraries can "follow the money" and gain new resources and services paid for outside their normal funding sources.** Foundations, government agencies, and corporations are receptive to programs and services which deal with adolescents, in particular in the areas of literacy, technology, employment, and increasing student learning and achievement. In particular, funding is available from a wide variety of sources to develop after-school programs in both school and public libraries. The funding streams are available because funders recognize what youth librarians have known for a long time, that libraries are a great place for teens to be. Many of the programs which have been honored by the Excellence in Library Service to Young Adults program sponsored by YALSA and funded by the Margaret Alexander Edwards Trust have been grant-funded programs.

If libraries collaborate with other agencies to provide after-school programs, they have responded to very real community needs. Finally, after-school programs give librarians who serve young adults, and the students who participate in them, a real chance to excel and "show off" their talents. After-school programs are just one example of services to young adults which result in positive outcomes for youth development and the library.

6. One reason that an after-school program for teens can have such a large impact relates back to the developmental needs of teenagers. The adolescent

years are a time of self-definition, a time when teens are making all sorts of major and minor life decisions. It is also a time when they are beginning to develop intellectually. It is a time when they start to stitch together a personal culture: the things they like to do with their time. **By serving teens, libraries help young adults define themselves as library users, as readers, as lifelong learners, and maybe even as library supporters.** If teens have the chance to be involved in the library, have the opportunity to learn skills, and have collections which speak to their needs, then the chances are great they will remain library users. The main thing they need to learn about libraries is not how to find a book or even how to successfully search the Internet; instead, **what teens need to learn is the value of libraries in their lives.** While they can learn this in public libraries without young adult librarians, or school libraries where the librarian is unable to provide a true program of services, the chances are much greater that teens will see the value in libraries when libraries show that they value teens by providing resources and services for them. If we want teens to value us, then we need to value them.

7. Just as important, another essential justification for serving teenagers is continuing the investment libraries have made in children's services and schools have made by stocking elementary school libraries full of books. Preschool story times, toddler programs, summer reading programs, and library "hour" are all fine programs. The goals of such programs are varied, but essentially they are efforts to help children form relationships with libraries, books, and learning. Yet, it is during the young adult years when that relationship is most seriously challenged and, thus, when resources are most needed and should be supplied, less are available. The relationship is challenged because students are becoming less focused on basic skills such as reading and because they are finding lots of other things to do with their recreational time other than reading. Other interests are pulling young people away from libraries as they leave elementary school. If there are no young adult services or strong secondary school libraries, then there is nothing to pull them back. **Serving young adults helps to guarantee that the investment made in children's services and elementary school libraries pays off.**

8. Another essential justification for serving young adults is again quite practical. High school is **the last opportunity for libraries to connect with groups of teens and teach them essential information literacy skills.** An organized program of instruction with the school library in the lead is the only way to ensure that no one graduates from high school without

an ability to locate, evaluate, and use information. Information literacy is not a luxury, but a core skill which will be required not just in higher education pursuits but in most any "good job." More than that, it is a life skill that can actually be taught in the classroom or library setting. "Learning across a lifetime, supported throughout our communities, is increasingly essential to a healthy and productive society." (Sheppard, 3) Without an organized program of information literacy instruction, schools will be sending students out into a world where they will not be able to compete. Instruction in information literacy, through teaching skills and encouraging independence, is a key to success. While an information literacy initiative is important in every setting, it is most crucial to those on the other side of the "digital bridge" who do not have ready access to computers. For many teenagers locked into poverty, high school may be their last opportunity to learn the information skills they will need to compete in the new economy.

9. Helping students succeed is a primary reason for providing quality library services to young adults. This is the goal of every school, of every parent, and of every community: to see that teens succeed in school. Library service to young adults supports student learning and achievement in every aspect of service. From the collections we build, to the services we offer, to the one-on-one reference assistance we provide, librarians support student success. By providing recreational reading, such as series books, we provide teens with materials that keep them reading. By providing access to the Internet, to databases, and to an entire collection of materials, we provide teens with the means to achieve in school. Librarians need to document these successes through stories and outcome statements from the teens themselves. As libraries position themselves as partners in the learning process, as we triumph in improving student learning and achievement, and as we plan services and develop collections that help students excel, then the public again has the value of libraries demonstrated to them. Libraries can demonstrate that they value what parents value: the success of their children in school.

10. Every organization has different reasons why it does not serve young adults with the same passion and same commitment of resources as it serves children and adults. There are always other priorities, but finding resources, externally or internally, to adequately fund services to young adults must become a priority in every school and public library. Why? Because **library service to young adults works; it is an efficient and even cost-effective method for libraries to serve this large user group.** The professional literature is filled with success stories of libraries that have dedicated

resources to serving young adults with great results, despite the dearth of long-range planning in these libraries. From large urban public libraries to suburban ones, from small rural libraries to secondary schools in every section of the country, when libraries dedicate resources to serve young adults they find the outcome is success for the library and its young adult customers. Young adults are better served and less often perceived as "trouble." Use of the library increases as measured by circulation, which assumes that reading also increases. Yet the primary outcome is that young adult services work for young adult customers. The services support their development into successful students and healthy adults.

Chapter 4

Two Roads to Travel

The visions and values provided in the earlier chapters are important building blocks in planning library service to young adults. Two publications that can be used as guides for further planning are the Public Library Association's *The New Planning for Results: A Streamlined Approach* (Nelson 2001) and the American Association of School Librarians' and the Association for Educational Communications and Technology's *Information Power: Building Partnerships for Learning* (AASL 1998). Together, the books provide information that can be combined by both school and public libraries to plan services and programs that will meet the unique developmental, informational, and recreational needs of young adults. Both have the common elements of vision and mission, goals, and objectives. But then their paths diverge—*The New Planning for Results* (NPFR) provides service responses and *Information Power: Building Partnerships for Learning* (IP2) provides a series of goals, some very broad and some very specific. Considered together, the commonalities are apparent, which indicates the importance of the need for collaboration among learning institutions in a community.

THE NEW PLANNING FOR RESULTS

With the emphasis on service responses, *The New Planning for Results* gives librarians planning for service to young adults a new perspective and a different outlook for their planning purposes. A service response is what a library does for, or offers to, the public in an effort to meet certain community needs. NPFR identifies thirteen possible service responses (appendix A).

NPFR suggests a planning process whereby, after determining community needs, public libraries select the service responses which best serve their community. **Each of these service responses has a strong young adult component.** Several, however, have particularly robust ties to service to young adults:

1. General information. A library that offers general information helps meet the need for information and answers to questions on a broad array of topics related to work, school, and personal life. Young adults are primary users of a school or public library's information services for all three reasons. Most young adults are students and need libraries to help them find information to complete homework assignments. The process of adolescence creates an interest in information related to personal life. Young adults are interested in answering questions about their "changing bodies, changing lives," as well using information services to help them obtain information for expanding personal interests. Finally, the work that most young adults do is going to school; thus, helping young adults find information for school *is* helping them with their work.

Equal access to information, in print and other formats, as well as equal access to services, is vital to successful service with young adults. Another key to success in this role is identifying and meeting the unique information needs of young adults. Libraries using this service response must meet the information needs of young adults through quality customer service, informational programming, outreach to schools, staff training in areas such as reference and readers' advisory, responsive collections, and the marketing of resources to young adult customers.

2. Current topics and titles. A library which provides current topics and titles helps fulfill community residents' appetite for information about popular culture and societal trends and their desire for satisfying recreational experiences. As teenagers are the prime movers in creating pop culture and trends, it is not surprising that young adults are primary consumers of popular materials, in particular popular fiction in paperback, magazines, and nonprint materials. Libraries which choose this role must meet the needs of young adults through quality customer services, involvement of youth in the collection development process, dedicated spaces, responsive collections, and the marketing of popular materials to young adult customers.

3. Formal learning support. A library that offers formal learning support helps students who are enrolled in a formal program of education or who are pursuing an education through a program of home-

schooling to attain their educational goals. User surveys repeatedly report that most young adults use the library to support their work in junior or senior high school. During the week the school library is most accessible, and on Saturday and Sunday afternoons, and evenings during the week in many public libraries, the majority of users are normally teens. The formal learning support may even extend to a programming response in the form of an after-school tutoring or homework help program. Public libraries, as documented by Cindy Mediavilla in *Creating the Full-Service Homework Center in Your Library* (2001), are actively involved in tutoring programs. Libraries choosing this service response must meet the needs of young adults through quality customer services, cooperation with school personnel, responsive collections, easy access to electronic resources, a strong reference collection, dedicated study spaces, hours conducive to young adult use, and the marketing of homework support services to young adult customers.

   4. Information literacy. A library that provides information literacy service helps address the need for skills related to finding, evaluating, and using information effectively. Spurred on by a wave of technology, this service response is one of the most important of all when serving young adults. In fact, the success of a library in this service response may determine success in a role such as formal education support and lifelong learning. By teaching young adult customers, through formal and informal means, how to access, evaluate, and use information, we are empowering youth. Given growing research about the lack of access to many young people, in particular poor and minority teens, urban and rural libraries must consider this a top priority. Seeking independence is one of the primary tasks which teens undergo as part of the life stage known as adolescence. Libraries can help teens by providing them with the skills and knowledge they need to become independent, responsible, and knowledgeable information consumers. Libraries which choose this response must meet the needs of young adults through collaboration with other learning institutions, quality customer services, easy access to electronic resources, a well-trained staff, a commitment to instruction, cooperation with school personnel, and the marketing of information literacy services to young adult customers.

   Information literacy is not library instruction. Just as youth development is a movement toward focusing on prevention rather then intervention, information literacy is focusing on learning as a process for solving information problems. **Information literacy is about teaching teens how to think as much as it is about teaching them how to do.** The resources many students are using are not found within the four walls of the library, but rather through the Internet. In a sense, information literacy is teaching young adults the basics of collection development. Just as we choose the best for students from the world of "real" materials, once we teach teenagers to be information literate, they will use similar criteria to choose the virtual materials to solve their information problem. **Information literacy is youth development in action; we are working *with* the students, not for them.**

If library instruction, in the world of card catalogs and the print version of *Readers' Guide to Periodical Literature*, was important, then in the Internet age teaching information literacy skills is vital. The Internet, and information technology generally, have dramatically changed the way young adults use libraries, for better and for worse. For the better, we actually find lots and lots of teens who are excited about research and about all the different formats in which they may find information. But with the excitement comes frustration because the increased opportunities to locate information no doubt overwhelm just as many young adults. There is so much information, so easily available, and all of it seemingly useful.

Information literacy teaches young adults the skills they need for completing research, but more importantly for solving any information problem, with the necessary skills to locate, evaluate, and use the information available to them. This skill, like the ability to write a paragraph or solve a math equation, becomes a basic skill for all students to master. **Like youth development, the focus of information literacy is building the assets within young people to help them make better choices.**

Information literacy also mirrors the youth development movement in its focus on building community. Central to information literacy is the idea of "learning community." The concept as described in IP2 is that everyone, not just students, is "interconnected in a lifelong quest to understand and meet . . . constantly changing information needs." **The goal of information literacy instruction is to ensure that young adults leave high school able to participate fully in this learning community.** Not surprisingly, the desired outcomes for information literate students are similar to those found in the youth development movement. According to *Information Literacy Standards for Student Learning* (see appendix H), students who are information literate can "become independent, ethical, lifelong learners who achieve personal satisfaction and who contribute responsibly and productively to the learning community and to society as a whole." In short, **information literacy creates healthy youth, which, in turn, creates a healthy community.**

5. Lifelong learning. A library that provides lifelong learning service helps address the desire for self-directed personal growth and development opportunities. Lifelong learning is an outgrowth of effective library service to young adults. If collections, programs, and other elements of the service responses reach the young adult user, the outcome will be to create a lifelong library user and perhaps a lifelong learner. Libraries that use this response must meet the lifelong learning needs of young adults through quality customer service, programming which promotes reading and library use, youth involvement at all levels including volunteers and youth advisory groups, equal access to materials and services, dedicated study spaces, hours conducive to young adult use, collaboration in the community with other youth serving agencies, and the marketing of these resources to young adult customers.

The other service responses, in particular cultural awareness, community information, and commons, can also play an important role in serving young adult customers. But it is these five service responses, in most libraries, that are the priorities. With teens, these are also the five main reasons they may use a library. Using these service responses along with the goals in IP2 provides a holistic point-of-view of library service to young adults.

INFORMATION POWER:
BUILDING PARTNERSHIPS FOR LEARNING

Just as the Public Library Association has identified primary service responses for public libraries in NPFR, the American Association of School Librarians has identified key goals for school libraries in IP2. Under each of these goals, there is great opportunity to expand services for young adults. While the goals, objectives, and tasks of the librarian working in a public library differ from the school library media specialist in a secondary school library, the vision is still the same, focusing on the outcome for teenagers to succeed in school and become well prepared to succeed in life. Working together within those areas of common interests such as adolescent literacy, youth participation, collection development, and information literacy, school library media specialists and public librarians have more shared goals than divergent paths.

For each IP2 goal, let's examine some possible service responses for school library media specialists serving young adults.

> To provide intellectual access to information through learning activities that are integrated into the curriculum and that help all students achieve information literacy by developing effective cognitive strategies for selecting, retrieving, analyzing, evaluating, synthesizing, creating, and communicating information in all formats and in all content areas of the curriculum

The primary service response is information literacy. Ideally, in a school setting, young adult students in all grades are provided with instruction that is integrated into the curriculum in solving information problems. While every school library media specialist approaches this goal differently, the key is to move away from the traditional library instruction model and practices where a certain grade of students in an English class come into the library on a given day to learn how to do research for their upcoming term paper. Instead, the instruction needs to take place throughout the curriculum and the grades so that students can build on basic information literacy skills and learn more complex skills. The key, especially with young adults, based on their developmental needs, is "active learning" that truly engages the young person in the process. The skills that teens employ in finding and using information, such as problem solving, are exactly the skills needed for other endeavors, including the taking of standardized tests. Information literacy needs to be seen not as an extra, but as a basic skill.

Working with young adults can be challenging, since many, if not most, are quite experienced, if not necessarily skilled, in using the Internet. In many ways, the instruction needs to focus not only on skills, but also on changing the culture of how teens think about information. For many young adults, it means moving them from the belief that typing two words into the more than one billion web pages available through a search engine is the most effective method to locate information. Teens think they know, but few really understand and possess, true information literacy skills. Information literacy instruction needs to build on the raw skills which most teens have and work toward refining them so students can truly succeed in solving information problems as they become more complex.

> To provide physical access to information through a carefully selected and systematically organized local collection of diverse learning resources that represent a wide range of subjects, levels of difficulty, and formats; a systematic procedure for acquiring information and materials from outside the library media center and the school through such mechanisms as electronic networks, interlibrary

loan, and cooperative agreements with other information agencies; and instruction in using a range of equipment for accessing local and remote information in any format

The service response of general information is a good fit with this goal. Given both the limited nature of most library budgets and the explosion of resources which are often only a click away, building a collection is no longer just a matter of acquiring resources, but also providing access to resources both inside and outside the library walls.

The wide range of young adult reading interests and reading levels presents a series of challenges when selecting materials. While looking at the holistic ways in which teens use libraries, librarians need to balance young adults' desire for recreational reading materials against the need to provide curriculum support. A high school library might have two biographies of the same person: one published by a library publisher, normally in a series, with a set number of pages, while the next will be a major work from a noted scholar published by a trade house. The public library may have two more. Two more might reside in a historical society or museum collections. Young adults should have access to any or all of them via interlibrary loan.

To provide learning experiences that encourage students and others to become discriminating consumers and skilled creators of information through comprehensive instruction related to the full range of communications media and technology

Lifelong learning is the service response most closely related to this goal. Libraries can empower young adults to become contributing members to the learning community as well as lifelong learners. Skills learned in school can be applied to jobs, careers, hobbies, and other interests when they are adults. Librarians can design assignments and projects where the final product utilizes the latest technology and is made available to a wider audience, such as a web page, a multimedia presentation, perhaps even streaming media. Librarians working with tech-savvy teens need to pay special attention to their own lifelong learning in order to keep pace with young adults. Libraries in the twenty-first century can become information meccas where students can learn and apply new methods of creating media and disseminating information. Librarians can teach classes, serve as advisors to technology clubs, or arrange mentoring programs to see that students gain the necessary skills, using the necessary tools, to become lifelong learners.

To provide leadership, collaboration, and assistance to teachers and others in applying principles of instructional design to the use of instructional and information technology for learning

Information literacy and lifelong learning are the service responses that match up best with this goal. The importance of collaboration, as well as the role of the school library media specialist as a partner in learning, is one of the central themes of IP2. Collaboration within a school and in the community is even more important when libraries are serving young adults. As the lives of students and their learning demands become more complex, it is vital that the school library be successfully integrated into the school's learning community and then make connections with other libraries in the community so that learning can be extended and enriched in the community. If the key to building assets is relationships, then the key to building partnerships also begins with relationships. From collaboration, synergy occurs. The best of what libraries can offer combined with the best of what the classroom offers will provide young adults with robust learning experiences. Librarians must demonstrate the successful elements to such partnerships, which in many ways are similar to those used in serving young adults. Partnerships occur when librarians are approachable, patient, persistent, flexible, committed to problem solving, and inclusive.

To provide resources and activities that contribute to lifelong learning while accommodating a wide range of differences in teaching and learning styles, methods, interests, and capacities

Again, the most closely related service response is lifelong learning. The importance of lifelong learning is clearly shown in this statement from *The Twenty-first Century Learner* (Sheppard 2001):

> The profound changes of the twenty-first century are transforming America into what must become a learning society. We enter this century in the midst of a bewildering mix of opportunity, uncertainty, challenge and change, all moving at unprecedented speed. Fueled by dazzling new technologies, increasing social diversity and divide, and radical shifts in industry and labor markets, accelerating change has become a way of life. To navigate the changes, minimize the risks and participate in shaping a new order, all Americans need access to learning throughout their lifetimes. Never before have museums, libraries, and the whole of the nonformal sector of educational institutions faced such challenges and opportunities. (2)

This notion of "learning across a lifetime" is increasingly essential to a healthy and productive society and needs to be supported across the community, not only in school and public libraries. Working with young adults, however, requires that the lifelong learning model be constantly reinforced because young adults tend to live "in the moment." Moreover, since not all learners learn at the same pace or with the same methods, there must be many access points for students. Technology is the key here since it more or less allows the user to choose his or her own level. Students can find the websites or database which best suits their needs once they have learned from their librarian the basics of finding, locating, and using information.

To provide a program that functions as the information center of the school, both through offering a locus for integrated and interdisciplinary learning activities within the school and through offering access to a full range of information for learning beyond this locus

General information is the service response of choice for this goal. In a school setting, the school library program must be positioned as the center of the learning community in the school so it is seen by students and faculty as the one point where all the strands of learning can come together. The public library can play the same role in the community. Librarians in both types of libraries can partner with teachers, provide technology, and increase student learning and achievement. They can also adopt a customer service approach to library service for young adults. One-on-one interaction with a person to help them solve an information problem, figure out how to use a particular database, or find a book to read is still a basic value of librarianship. The library becomes the true center of learning for students when it is a place they value because the staff there values them. When reference services, readers' advisory interviews, and the enforcement of appropriate behavior are delivered with a proactive customer service attitude, the chances increase that the student will see the library as we see it—important and of value. When students learn that library staff value them as individuals, value their input and ideas and energy and even independence, then the value of the library will increase in their eyes.

To provide resources and activities for learning that represent a diversity of experiences, opinions, and social and cultural perspectives and to support the concept that intellectual freedom and access to information are prerequisite to effective and responsible citizenship in a democracy

The service response most suitable here is current topics and titles. Young adults entering libraries in most schools are a much more culturally diverse group than those who entered ten or even five years ago. Given the changing nature of library users, and given the knowledge that services mirror the needs of the community, librarians must adapt in many areas, but primarily in collection development. From young adult fiction which speaks to particular ethnic background and situations to the vast resources of the Internet, libraries are perfectly positioned to be the drivers of diversity.

CONTINUING TO PLAN

Planning library services never occurs in a vacuum. The service responses in NPFR and the goals in IP2 provide excellent models and ideas for developing services for young adults. In both environments, serving young adults needs to be positioned within the overall vision and mission of the institution. The direction for services to young adults is guided first by the needs of teens. To gain necessary support, the directions must follow the path of overall library or school planning. The capacity of a library to actually meet these goals or fulfill these service responses certainly varies with funding, size of library, number of staff, and the amount of administrative support received. The quality of the services, of course, will depend on establishing a clear vision, following core values, responding to the real needs of teenagers, and developing service responses and goals that achieve the desired results of increasing learning and achievement and supporting healthy youth development.

Chapter 5

Itinerary for Quality Library Services to Young Adults

After developing a strategic plan for service to young adults based on the fundamental values, and after combining service responses in the NPFR and the goals in IP2, librarians working with young adults can then begin to develop specific strategies and services that will implement this plan. They will have to decide where to focus and how to effectively allocate resources to achieve the desired results. While every library serving teens will have a different complement of resources to choose from, libraries in almost any setting have seven action areas in common:

> Administration
> Collections
> Programs
> Services
> Electronic resources
> Facilities and hours
> Staff

The allocation of these resources hinges on many factors, but the one overriding factor is meeting the overall needs of the library. If a successful program of service to young adults is creative, dynamic, and cutting edge, it will contribute to the overall needs of the institution. If it is not effective, then the program is at-risk for losing support. Allocating resources is the manifestation of priority setting.

If all the strategies listed below are provided by a library, a high level of quality service to young adults has been achieved. The checklist can be used to plan for service and to evaluate service in each of the action areas listed above. No library can, or perhaps should, respond in each area to the depth or breadth suggested in these strategies; instead, the checklist serves as a direction, not as standard or requirement. The only standard for serving young adults is that resources are allocated in a manner which responds to the needs of the young adult customer, results in positive youth development, and supports the results of student learning and achievement.

ADMINISTRATION

_____ Provides programs, services, and resources suitable to the developmental needs of young adults and to the principles of positive youth development

_____ Develops **an overall plan of services for young adults,** based on youth involvement, that speaks to the holistic manner in which young adults use schools and public libraries

_____ Employs young adult specialists in the public library setting and a certified school library media specialist in the school library who are charged with the planning, development, implementation, and evaluation of programs and services

_____ Provides sufficient support staff to provide quality service

_____ Involves young adults in planning and decision-making throughout the library

_____ Provides a **robust budget** to fund programs and services that is in proportion to resources dedicated to services for children and adults and, in the school library setting, a budget which allows the school library media specialist to fulfill the school's goals for student learning and achievement

_____ **Maintains budget lines** to support services and collections

_____ Maintains records and statistics that enable the library to **evaluate** young adult services on a regular basis

_____ Makes a commitment to include service to young adults as an **integral part of the institution's mission, goals, objectives, and strategic planning**

_____ Provides a **unique and identifiable area in the institution** that is dedicated to young adults that serves as the focal point for services

_____ Upholds the **value of equal access** to buildings, resources, programs, and services for young adults

_____ Provides **quality customer service** to young adults that is demonstrated by staff at every service point

_____ Ensures that staff are approachable and nonjudgmental, and that they treat young adults with respect and courtesy

_____ Builds assets with services that demonstrate the library's commitment to the needs of the community

_____ Provides equal access to **young adults** in age-specific policies

_____ Supports **intellectual freedom** and the concept of free and equal access for young adults

_____ Develops and adopts **written policies** on selection, copyright, challenges, confidentiality, Internet use, behavior, use of services and facilities, and intellectual freedom that mandate the rights of young adults

_____ **Evaluates service to young adults** as part of the institution's ongoing planning and evaluation process

_____ Develops and adopts **policies related to patron behavior** that do not single out or discriminate against young adults

_____ Ensures that boards of trustees, school boards, administrators, and directors understand, value, and demonstrate through their actions their support of service to young adults

_____ Develops and implements **specific goals and objectives** to underscore the institution's commitment to service to young adults

_____ **Supports all types of partnerships that will benefit young adult users.** Partnerships may take many shapes, some merely involving shared communication, while others demonstrate true collaboration in action at all levels.

COLLECTIONS

_____ Integrates the collection for young adults into the **library's overall collection development plan and policy**

_____ Views **collection development for young adults holistically;** collects materials outside those directly written and marketed for young adults that may be of use to young adult customers

_____ Develops and maintains active collections of **print young adult fiction** titles, in particular those which speak to the issues of cultural awareness and diversity, those that have received awards, and those that are accessible to reluctant readers

_____ Develops and maintains active collections **of print paperback reprints and originals,** in particular, series books which meet the recreational reading interests of younger teens

_____ Develops and maintains collections of **graphic novels** to serve the diverse reading interests of teen users, in particular to provide a format of interest to male readers

_____ Develops and maintains a strong selection of **adult fiction titles of interest to teens,** in particular in the genres of science fiction, fantasy, and horror. Popular best-sellers, as well as classics, both established and contemporary or cult favorites, will meet the reading needs of older teens.

_____ Develops and maintains a collection of **audio books,** in part to meet the needs of young adult customers who are new to reading in the English language, suffer from a reading disability, or simply listening to books on tape

_____ Develops and maintains print nonfiction collections. These **nonfiction collections focus on popular and informational materials,** particularly in the areas of popular culture, health and sexuality, self-help or popular psychology, and materials related to college and careers.

_____ Develops and **maintains nonfiction print collections which support the formal education needs of students,** including multiple copies of books for required reading assignments

_____ Develops and **maintains nonfiction print collections which support the wide range of reading levels of young adults**

_____ Develops and maintains **nonfiction print collections which support student learning,** such as test guides and study aids

_____ Develops and maintains, with the assistance of young adult customers, **a collection of popular music,** in a variety of formats

_____ Develops and maintains **collections of CD-ROMs** to be checked out or used in the library, which support the recreational, educational, and informational needs of teenagers

_____ Develops a collection of **visual information,** in formats such as video and DVD. Visual formats support the media savvy young adult consumer, as well as being easily accessible for young adults new to reading in the English language. Depending upon the setting, visual formats may include recreational materials (skateboarding, movies, sports), informational (study guides, health information), and educational (biographies, history, and other curriculum-related subjects).

_____ Develops a collection of **magazines.** Magazines need to be both of broad popular interest, as well as support niche interest. Titles should include those written and marketed for teens, as well as selected titles created for adults but with high interest to teenagers, in particular in the areas of sports, computer gaming, and popular culture.

_____ Develops a collection of **comic books.** Comic books provide reading materials for reluctant readers, in particular, boys. In addition, they take up little room, cost little, and are self-weeding.

_____ Develops and maintains collections, where appropriate, of materials for young adults in **languages other than English**

_____ **Develops collections of print and nonprint materials which respond to trends and fads,** in particular in the areas of popular culture

_____ Improves access to collections by working with teachers and librarians to **better understand the formal educational needs of students**

_____ Develops **numerous and diverse methods to communicate with teachers and other librarians** more effectively and efficiently

_____ Develops methods to **involve youth in the collection development process,** such as reading interest surveys, magazine or music selection groups, or genre selection committees

_____ Develops an aggressive strategy of **weeding the collection** to provide maximum exposure to new titles and space to display materials

_____ Supports reading programs and initiatives, such as Teen Read Week, which **promote adolescent literacy**

_____ Improves use of collections through a **targeted marketing campaign** aimed at students. All aspects of this campaign should be planned, implemented, and evaluated by young adults.

_____ Develops methods for **measuring the use of all collections.** Data should be collected to allow for analysis by use of materials *for* young adults and use of materials *by* young adults.

_____ Develops collections and services that **increase access to the library and its collections for young adults who do not have transportation to a public library.** Services might include books by mail, delivery service to or from schools, or youth-serving agencies.

_____ Utilizes other youth-serving organizations as **distribution channels** for library resources through the use of deposit collections, special exhibits, special events, extended loan periods, and library visits

_____ Develops a wide range of materials, such as print book lists or links from a young adult web page, which provide young adults with **improved access to the collection and other sources of information to encourage reading**

_____ Develops and maintains collections that follow the **best practices of merchandising** to display the collection and arouse the interest of users

_____ Subscribes to the key reviewing journals in the field, including *Booklist, Voice of Youth Advocates, Kliatt Paperback Book Guide,* and *School Library Journal,* as well as paying attention to books and media reviewed in popular media, such as *Teen People* and *Seventeen*

PROGRAMS (PROGRAMS IN THIS SECTION REFER TO INDIVIDUAL EVENTS AND ACTIVITIES)

_____ Plans programs **within the framework of the strategic plan** and not in isolation

_____ Develops and presents programs based on developmental needs, positive youth development concepts, and developmental assets

_____ Develops and presents a **wide range of programs for young adults with young adult involvement from planning to evaluation,** through the use of surveys, focus groups, and advisory groups

_____ Develops and presents programs which **provide young adults with creative outlets,** such as art programs, creative writing programs, and drama programs. By encouraging the creativity of young adults, libraries are not only promoting use of collections, but also building assets.

_____ Develops and presents **programs which create community** among young adults, allow for social interaction, and give young adults a sense of belonging and bonding to libraries

_____ Develops and presents **programs to promote use of the resources of the library**

_____ Delivers programs to young adults in **"nontraditional" settings,** where audiences could be young adults who are home-schooled, enrolled in alternative education programs, homeless, housed in residential care or treatment facilities, or detained in juvenile detention facilities

_____ Designs and manages a comprehensive **program (personnel, resources, facility, and services) of information literacy instruction** and practice in the use of information. Guidance should be given for reading, viewing, and listening so that students can locate resources for both personal enrichment as well as for information problem solving.

_____ Develops and manages **after-school programs** which offer tutoring, information literacy instruction, and other activities to bond young adults with books, libraries, and learning

_____ Develops **programs which allow young adults to respond to their reading,** such as book discussion groups

_____ Develops **programs that speak to the informational needs of young adults** in areas such as college and career information and health information, as well as personal enrichment

_____ Develops programs that **speak to the recreational needs of young adults,** in particular in areas which support or promote the library's resources

SERVICES

_____ Develops and offers **reference and information services** for young adults which provide a positive experience for the customer

_____ Develops and offers **proactive reference services,** such as homework collections or pathfinders, which allow young adults to work independently

_____ Develops and implements **customer service practices** which seek to assist young adults in finding information, such as staff working one-on-one with a teenager at a library computer

_____ Develops and implements customer services interactions for young adults, at all service points that **reflect the traits of respect, approachability, helpfulness, open-mindedness, sense of humor, and empathy.** Young adults are viewed by all staff as customers to be served, not problems to be solved or patrons to be "coped" with.

_____ Develops and offers **readers' advisory services** which nurture a young adult reader's relationship with books and with library staff

_____ **Designs and offers learning activities** which enhance the classroom experience, teach information literacy skills, and engage young adults in the learning process

_____ Develops and manages services that **utilize the skills, talents, and resources of young adults** in the school or community

_____ Develops and supervises formal **youth participation programs,** such as a teen advisory group

_____ Develops and offers opportunities **which allow young adults to participate** in groups such as the Friends of the Library, the library board, and the school library advisory committee

_____ Develops and manages services **based on the Search Institute's Developmental Assets model** to demonstrate support for positive youth development

_____ Develops and manages services that **reduce the frustration of young adults** when they use libraries

_____ Develops and manages services which allow **school classes to make frequent visits** to the library for educational, informational, and recreational reasons

_____ Develops and manages **services with a variety of partners** including classroom teachers, club advisors, coaches, school counselors, parents, and other members of the larger learning community

_____ Develops **services with youth-serving groups** in the field of recreation, alternative education, and human services

_____ Develops and manages services that meet the unique educational needs of the **home-schooled young adult**

_____ Develops **relationships with teachers and other librarians as partners to collaborate in the planning, design, delivery, and evaluation of instruction in information literacy skills** using a variety of resources and problem-solving skills

_____ Serves as a resource expert and a consultant when teachers are making the **transition from textbook-centered instruction to resource-based instruction**

_____ Partners with teachers to **empower students** to accept responsibility for their own learning, thereby becoming capable of learning over a lifetime

ELECTRONIC RESOURCES

_____ Develops and maintains **web pages which support the formal educational needs of students.** These should include links to library catalogs, databases, and selected quality Internet links in order to increase the efficiency and effectiveness of information searches for library staff, teachers, parents, and young adult customers.

_____ Develops and maintains **web pages which support the needs of teens for information on current topics and general information,** in particular, in areas of personal interest such as college and career information

_____ Develops and offers programs, user tools, online tutorials, and web pages that support the need for an **information literate** young adult

_____ **Develops and maintains all web content with young adults involved** in planning, implementation, and evaluation

_____ **Develops and maintains web pages which support interactivity,** such as surveys, polls, and other methods to gather information directly from young adult customers

_____ Develops and oversees technology-based **interactive services,** such as e-mail reference, chat-based reference, or Instant Message-based reference

_____ Develops and uses effective **measures to manage Internet and other electronic resources** that provide young adult users with equal access

_____ Develops **programming related to electronic resources** to help "move" Internet-only users into other library services and collections. Programs might include web camps, Internet-based tutoring, web CE, and other projects that utilize the library's electronic resources.

_____ Provides **leadership, expertise, and advocacy** in the use of electronic resources at the school, building, district, or system level

_____ Develops a **marketing plan** to increase awareness and use of the library's electronic resources

_____ **Networks the library's resources** within the institution and with other learning institutions to allow access to resources from home as well as from a school or library

_____ Develops criteria for the selection of electronic resources including **databases** that will support student learning and achievement

FACILITIES AND HOURS

_____ Establishes **areas** that include collections, electronic resources, and seating

_____ Establishes areas with differentiated spaces for a variety of types of activities while offering a **degree of privacy** with clear sightlines for supervision

_____ Defines areas using effective signage or other directional devices

_____ Creates an **inviting environment** through appropriate lighting, seating, and décor that welcomes young adults and makes them feel comfortable

_____ Provides **adequate fixtures and space to display materials** in order to practice bookstore-style merchandising to promote collections

_____ Provides **areas for free materials,** including local newspapers, zines, and informational items from youth-serving agencies

_____ Utilizes **public library meeting room spaces** to expand services and programs that include study times, recreational programs, after-school programming, and tutoring/mentoring activities

_____ **Develops teen friendly signage** in all parts of the library, in particular in the nonfiction areas, for ease of access. Signs should be, where appropriate, in languages other than English.

_____ Provides **multiple computers for Internet access,** as well as those with access to library catalogs and databases

_____ Provides **multiple computers which have access to educational and recreational CD-ROM software, word processing, and** other information resources

_____ Develops **spaces** which include laptop plug-in stations, listening and viewing stations, coffee bars, a copying room, and a variety of study spaces for individuals and groups, and increased small group study areas

_____ Opens **hours that are "in synch" with teen lives.** Young adult surveys repeatedly state the need for longer hours in libraries. Later hours, at least during exam times, should also be considered.

_____ **Develops effective outreach services** from the library to other institutions and organizations, in particular in the areas of booktalking to promote reading and information literacy instruction. Outreach is an effective and efficient method to provide a high level of service in a short amount of time. It does not require increasing the library's hours, but may require creative staffing arrangements.

_____ **Offers service at times when the library or institution in which it is housed is usually closed.** Opening on Friday evenings, Sunday afternoons, and during school vacations will demonstrate a more efficient use of library resources and facilities and benefit young adults as well.

_____ **Designs facilities to meet study needs,** including a mix of study carrels, computer stations, and individual, small group, and large group seating arrangements

_____ Designs facilities to **meet the recreational needs** of teens, including areas for viewing videos, DVDs, cable television, or other visual media. The space would include areas for listening to music or audiobooks, in formats including tapes, compact discs, and MP3.

_____ Allows librarians working with young adults sufficient **off-desk time** to plan and develop services, do outreach into schools and the community, and attend meetings to network with other youth-serving agencies

_____ Develops **schedules to ensure time for teachers and librarians and others in the learning community to meet on a regular basis** to coordinate planning, development, implementation, and evaluation of programs and services that support learning, provide positive youth development experiences, and build assets in the community

_____ Designs facilities to **accommodate classes** and provides ample room for resources, as well as areas for students to utilize resources, such as a media lab, computer center, or production space

STAFF

_____ Provides **training through the use of YALSA Serving the Underserved trainers** (appendix C) so that all staff will be prepared to provide quality service to young adults. Training is offered on an ongoing regular basis and is integrated within the library's training program.

_____ **Assigns the most qualified staff member** to provide service to young adults when there is no specialist or certified staff member

_____ Develops **continuing education** for staff in a variety of areas, such as collection development, behavior management, program development, and reading promotion

_____ Develops and manages a program to **recruit and place teen volunteers** through improved communication with school service learning personnel and other entities providing community service volunteers

_____ Develops and manages a program to **hire young adults to work in libraries,** to perform a wide variety of tasks

_____ Develops methods to **mentor, retain, and promote** young adult workers so they can meet their educational goals

_____ Develops and manages a program to **better utilize teen volunteers** through improved training and sharing of knowledge among staff to ensure meaningful work for young adult volunteers

_____ Develops and oversees **mentoring programs** that allow older young adults to work one-on-one with younger young adults to increase student achievement

_____ Develops effective methods of **internal communication,** such as a monthly e-newsletter, to increase awareness of young adult services

_____ Maintains a **commitment to individualized professional development** through the encouragement of staff to read professional literature, subscribe to electronic discussion lists, and to read widely about young adults in the popular press

_____ Develops **employment opportunities for young adults,** in particular in the substitute capacity to allow for flexibility in scheduling

_____ Develops **funding resources to acquire additional staffing resources,** in particular project-based funding with definable outcomes, which provides paid work for young adults themselves

_____ Maintains **a reasonable ratio of professional staff to young adult client populations** in the school and in the community in order to provide for adequate levels of quality service

_____ Advocates for a **young adult specialist in each public library building.** Research supports a greater quantity and higher quality of service to young adults when a young adult specialist is on staff.

_____ Provides an **adequate number of support staff** in each library

_____ Develops and maintains an **open and flexible schedule** in the school library. Students and teachers must be able to come to libraries throughout the day to use information sources, to read for pleasure, and to meet and work with each other.

_____ Develops **collaborative strategies for working with other libraries and learning institutions** to provide positive youth development activities, meet the developmental needs of adolescents, and build assets in the community

_____ Offers **staff development opportunities** that allow librarians working with teens to continue their education through workshop and conference attendance, participation on local or national committees, as well as other opportunities to gain knowledge of skills related to serving youth

_____ **Uses the competencies** established in the "Young Adults Deserve the Best: Competencies for Librarians Serving Young Adults" (YALSA 1994) to guide staff development opportunities (see appendix J)

_____ Assists in local, state, and national efforts to **recruit librarians,** in particular into the fields of youth services and school librarianship

_____ Develops **mentoring programs to assist new librarians** entering the field

_____ Works to **retain librarians serving young adults** by providing leadership opportunities, opportunities for promotion, and institutional support

Implementing these strategies in the key action areas of the library will go a long way toward ensuring quality library service to young adults. As the strategies are prioritized and resources allocated, these actions will begin to make the vision of services to young adults real. Each library will develop a different complement of strategies based on its resources and the young adults it serves, but all are directed at the outcome of increased student learning and achievement and the support of healthy youth development.

Chapter 6

Reaching the Destination: Success Stories

Building on core values, this book has described a planning process, a rationale, and strategies that will provide new directions for libraries. The focus is on an overall strategic plan for service to young adults, not on specific areas such as young adult literature or booktalking or teaching information skills. The book's focus is on the "big picture."

This chapter focuses on the images that make up the "big picture." It's about what librarians working with teens do every day. It puts the philosophy of *Directions* to work. These success stories demonstrate the value of library service to young adults based on adolescent needs, positive youth development, and developmental assets that result in positive outcomes for teenagers.

JANA FINE, a past president of the Young Adult Library Services Association and young adult librarian at the Clearwater Public Library in Florida, demonstrates the core values by:

> Working with professionals in schools and community organizations to further the rights of and opportunities for teens
>
> Presenting public programs that highlight programs of interest to teens. These programs are presented by teens themselves and reach out to others who come in contact with teens in their daily work or lives

MARY HENNESSEY, young adult librarian at the East Lansing Public Library in Michigan:

Realizes that many adults think negatively of teens so she tries to show the community the good things that teens are capable of by using teen volunteers in the library. The volunteers have taken on lots of different tasks from shelving books to helping with children's crafts to decorating the young adult room.

Created the Excellence in Library Services to Young Adults award-winning Stories in the Garden program as a way to get teens involved in the community and to show the community how caring and talented young adults can be.

AMBER TONGATE, the library media specialist at the Martin Luther King Jr. Academy in Lexington, Kentucky:

Promotes reading aloud through the RAT (Reading Aloud Teachers) Patrol. Each Friday during the school year, she hosts a drawing to see who will be a member of the RAT Patrol. Any teacher who has read aloud to his or her class for at least ten minutes that day can be nominated by student patrol members who receive a badge to hang on the door to their classroom.

Provided her school with more than $25,000 worth of books by winning the Young Adult Library Services Association's Great Book Giveaway in a school where teachers had brought books from their homes, garage sales, and other schools and stacked them together on one wall in the computer lab to create a "library."

VICTORIA VANNUCCI, the young adult librarian at the Cleveland Heights–University Heights Public Library in Ohio:

Created a small creative writing magazine using poetry and fiction submissions from local teens to encourage teenagers to express themselves on paper

Created a program entitled Reading Heroes, pairing older children (10-19) with younger children (entering second or third grade). The goal of the program was to develop and model a love of reading for younger children. Reading Heroes not only helped prepare younger children for the school year, it also provided teens with an opportunity to contribute to the community and the experience of making a difference in the life of a child.

ELIZABETH GALLAWAY, the young adult librarian at the Haverhill Public Library in Massachusetts:

> Networks with other youth providers by attending meetings of the Haverhill Teen Coalition, an agency of youth and adult volunteers whose mission is to improve the health and safety of young people. The library participated in the coalition's spring scavenger hunt this year.

> Developed the library's Cyber Center with the participation of a teen task force which was central to the room design, planning, and mission statement. The center hosts fifteen unfiltered computers for research, chat, e-mail, games, and web design. A guided access home page directs teens to carefully selected and reviewed age-appropriate links, many of which are recommended by teens. The center began a volunteer program where forty teens take turns staffing the room two to four hours a week and assist computer users of all ages.

JENNIFER HUBERT, a middle school library media specialist at the Little Red School House in New York:

> Created "Open Mic Nite," based on teen input, where teens perform in the library's auditorium with a local DJ providing the music. Every person who performs receives a T-shirt.

> Worked with a high school for pregnant teens and teen moms, visiting the school's day-care center once a month during the school year and doing a lap-sit story time with the teen moms and their babies. Hubert made handouts of nursery rhymes and took stacks of board books, which the moms read when she was done with the music and rhymes.

SHEILA ANDERSON, a young adult librarian at the Allen County Public Library in Fort Wayne, Indiana:

> Manages a homework-help drop-in program for middle and high school students who need help with their homework. Volunteers help the students, mostly with math and science. The library works with the school systems in the county in order to attract students to the program.

> Coordinates the Teen Agency Program (TAP), which provides special collections of paperback books to six area youth centers, juvenile

detention centers, and group homes. The TAP outreach effort also includes booktalking and involvement in the library's young adult summer reading program.

PAULA BREHM-HEEGER, a youth services librarian at Trails West Branch of the Kansas City (Missouri) Public Library:

> Created a successful book discussion group for teens from 13 to 17. The Friends of the Kansas City Public Library approved enough funds so that paperback books could be purchased for the discussion meetings. The teens get to keep these books. A local restaurant owner supplies pizza each month for the meeting at a large discount.

> Empowers the teens in her council, for example, by asking them to create a display for the teen bulletin board. Providing general direction and supplies, Brehm-Heeger saw the teens jump into action as they decided on the theme of the bulletin board, "Why I like teen council at the library."

NANCI MILONE-HILL, the head of young adult services at the Peabody Institute Public Library in Massachusetts:

> Partners with Cablevision's community access station to produce *Teen Talk*, a cable television show. The teens that participate in this teen issue program decide on the topics that will be discussed; they also build the set and do all of the taping and editing. They have had discussions on teen pregnancy, school violence, the new teen driving regulations, parent-child power struggles, and teen drinking. The shows are run on the community access channel for the city.

> Partners with the adult services librarian to run a mother/daughter book discussion group, which has been expanded to include Peabody teachers with their students. As a result of their participation in this discussion group, several teachers have become great advocates for this program and for the library.

MELISSA ORTH, a young adult librarian at the Curtis Memorial Library in Maine:

> Created a teen advisory board to assist in all aspects of developing a service program, beginning with a three-hour brainstorming session

where teens filled an easel pad full of ideas about programs, collections, and services.

Revamped the young adult space, making it more teen friendly through aggressive weeding, input from the teen board, and using funky decorations.

MARI HARDACRE, the young adult services manager at the Carmel Clay Public Library and **CONNIE MITCHELL**, media specialist, Carmel High School in Indiana:

Collaborated on a successful program in honor of National Poetry Month, "Poetry Wrap Up!" With help from teen decorators, the public library's program room took on a coffeehouse ambiance. Open mic segments were interspersed with spontaneous writing segments—scrawled on place mats—on topics that included who am I?; zoo animals; romance; states of mind; frustrations; and more. A highlight of the evening was two freshmen girls performing "Long Live the Pasty Book Nerds!" which has become the young adult department theme-poem: "Dear sweet library/our second home/we've had almost every book on loan/we are the pasty book nerds . . . ."

JANE BAIRD, the young adult coordinator at the Anchorage Public Library in Alaska:

Created, in cooperation with a local high school counselor, a "college application seminar" designed for junior or senior students actively applying for college. Some of the topics discussed were: where to apply; how to apply; from whom to get letters of recommendation; how to apply for financial aid; and good "hooks" for writing essays.

Developed the "Food and Film Festival," where, over a four-month period, a movie was shown in the library's public conference room, which has an attached kitchen. During intermission, teens retired to the kitchen and made food based on the film being shown.

NICK BURON, the young adult coordinator for the Queens Borough Public Library in New York:

Oversees the library's Teen Empowerment project, which serves as an alternative to punishment and a community service for teens enrolled in the Second Chance program, a program comprised of young people who have pleaded guilty to low-level misdemeanors. In cooperation with the district attorney's office, the library offers at-risk teens, ages 16-19, career counseling, workshops, library cards cleared of fines, computer training, book discussions, college scholarship information, and armed forces information. The project is designed to change negative behavior into positive behavior. It encourages teens to develop the skills necessary to become productive members of society and to take control of how they live their lives.

SUE MELLOTT, youth services librarian for the North Regional Library in Burlington, North Carolina:

> Organized a teen group called the Coffee Crew which packs food for Meals-on-Wheels (a community agency that distributes food to the elderly who are confined to their homes).

> Participated in collaborative projects with the local Boys and Girls Clubs in the community. The teens painted pumpkins and donated them to the clubs, put on a Christmas party, and are in the process of planning a Summer Bash for the club members. The teens also recently participated in the program, Love Letters to Cancer Patients.

DIANE TUCCILLO, a young adult librarian for the Mesa Public Library in Arizona:

> Developed *FRANK*, a magazine of original teen poetry, stories, essays, and art work published annually. A teen volunteer editorial board meets regularly to select pieces for the magazine and put it all together. Teens can sign up for the editorial board (and are considered official library volunteers) or submit work for consideration. The magazine is sold at the library Friends' desk for fifty cents, and proceeds go to help pay for other library youth programs. Complimentary reading copies are sent to all the junior and senior high school libraries, and a reading copy is also available in all three branch YA magazine collections. This is an opportunity for teens to see their work in print, to share their ideas and feelings with other teens, to encourage other teens to read and write, and to promote the library through their work.

JO-ANN CARHART, head of adult and young adult services for the East Islip Public Library in New York:

> Organized a YA drama group that performs for children in the library and in other locations in the community. The group dramatizes children's books, poems, and songs. It also conducts a costume parade of the children during intermission. The teens have a chance to be creative, show off their talents, and also contribute to the community. They promote literacy and the library, but mostly they promote the idea of teens using their talents to give back to the community.

EVIE WILSON-LINGBLOOM, a branch manager for the Sno-Island System in Washington:

> Created an urban legends collaborative project with teachers and librarians. The YA public librarian works with teachers and media specialists to schedule a brief presentation of teenage urban legends. This presentation is *very* interactive because every student has a story from his or her culture. Often students who rarely speak in class are the first to share their stories. Following the visit by the YA librarian, the teacher or librarian plans an activity in which the students write and present additional legends and folklore. Not only are the rewards for teens and librarians significant, but this program is also more cost-effective than a standard booktalking presentation which requires much more preparation.

JEFFIE NICHOLSON, a librarian for the Williamson County Public Library in Tennessee:

> Created a Teen Open House program where the library is open one Saturday evening a month for the Second Saturday coffeehouse (barring holiday conflicts). Local teen bands provide the entertainment. The library provides light snacks (chips, coffee, cokes) and staff are available to assist as needed (checking books in and out, doing reference, computer assistance, etc.).

The eighteen success stories here are typical of the ways in which librarians serving young people between the ages of 12 and 18 put their values into action. By working with youth, respecting their needs, collaborating with others who serve youth, by ensuring equal access and by focusing on programs and services that contribute to healthy youth development, these librarians have made a difference. They are not exceptions, but merely examples of those doing stellar work in school and public libraries in the United States.

The professional literature, in particular in the pages of the *Journal of Youth Services in Libraries* and *Voice of Youth Advocates* as well as the messages posted on the various YALSA-sponsored discussion lists, shows that "YA Works."

Most of these librarians work in small library systems, many are "lone rangers"; one (Orth) is not just the only young adult librarian in her system, but also the only one in the entire state. But all of them planned their services and took them in new directions. In doing so, they ensured teens positive outcomes by offering a holistic program of service that not only spoke to what teens said they wanted, but also responded to their developmental needs. They moved teens from the margins of library service and taught them about the value of libraries in their lives. Through collections, programs, services, technology, youth involvement, and collaboration these librarians have contributed to the healthy development of youth, the ultimate outcome of library service to young adults.

Chapter 7

A Successful Journey: Outcomes

Why should libraries follow these new directions? This map? This itinerary? What will the outcomes be if they "buy in" to the latest guidelines for library services to young adults? What is in it for them? What is in it for young adults? What are the expected outcomes for the communities where the library and the young adults reside?

Possible outcomes for the library include

Positioning as a major youth-serving organization in the community

Recognition as a "major player" in the youth development movement

More opportunities to apply for grants and other types of funding

Greater visibility because of service provided to a "high profile" segment of society

Involvement in the adolescent literacy and information literacy movement

More support for new buildings, bond issues, and funding

Additional allies in the defense of equal access and intellectual freedom

Possible outcomes for young adults are

More self-confidence because of their involvement in library programs and services

The acquisition of a sense of responsibility

A commitment to the library and its use

Development of the habit of lifelong learning

Knowledge about librarianship as a career

Feeling a part of something larger than themselves

Providing a service in the community

Developing high levels of reading, writing, and thinking skills

Sense of safety in their environment

Positive relationships with peers and adults

Developing social skills

The outcomes for the community might include

Involving a large segment of their population (young adults) in their discussion and decision-making which adds to the richness of civic dialogue

Involving young adults in planning, implementation, and evaluation of programs which means a more economical use of funds

Adding young adults to the labor force builds the pool of workers in the community

Taking advantage of more funding opportunities for community-wide efforts to provide positive youth development activities

Utilizing young adults as volunteers to serve the community

Developing more positive images of young adults

When we follow these new directions, we realize the value of our own work. It is not about selecting books or planning programs—those are merely tasks we do. Taking this journey and placing what librarians working with teens do everyday into this larger context remind us of the true value of the work we do which is helping kids and the community become more successful. It is a direction that builds assets, realizes outcomes, and supports healthy youth development.

Service Responses from
*The New Planning for Results:
A Streamlined Approach*

Basic literacy addresses the need to read and to perform other essential daily tasks.

Business and career information addresses a need for information related to business, careers, work, entrepreneurship, personal finances, and obtaining employment.

Commons addresses the need of people to meet and interact and to engage in public discourse about community issues.

Community referral addresses the need for public information related to services provided by community agencies and organizations.

Consumer information helps to satisfy the need for information to make informed consumer decisions and to help residents become more self-sufficient.

Cultural awareness helps satisfy the desire of community residents to gain an understanding of their own cultural heritage and the cultural heritage of others.

Current topics and titles help the community residents' appetite for information about popular cultural and social trends and their desire for satisfying recreational experiences.

Formal learning support helps students who are enrolled in a formal program of education or who are pursuing their education through a program of home-schooling to attain their educational goals.

General information helps meet the need for information and answers to questions on a broad array of topics related to work, school, and personal life.

Government information helps satisfy the need for information about elected officials and government agencies that enables people to participate in the democratic process.

Information literacy helps address the need for skills related to finding, evaluating, and using information effectively.

Lifelong learning helps address the desire for self-directed personal growth and development opportunities.

Local history and genealogy address the desire of community residents to know and better understand personal or community heritage.

The 40 Developmental Assets

	CATEGORY	ASSET NAME AND DEFINITION	
EXTERNAL ASSETS	**Support**	1. Family support	Family life provides high levels of love and support.
		2. Positive family communication	Young person and her or his parent(s) communicate positively, and young person is willing to seek advice and counsel from parent(s).
		3. Other adult relationships	Young person receives support from three or more nonparent adults.
		4. Caring neighborhood	Young person experiences caring neighbors.
		5. Caring school climate	School provides a caring, encouraging environment.
		6. Parent involvement in schooling	Parent(s) are actively involved in helping young person succeed in school.

Used with permission of the Search Institute

(continued)

EXTERNAL ASSETS

CATEGORY	ASSET NAME AND DEFINITION	
Empowerment	7. Community values youth	Young person perceives that adults in the community value youth.
	8. Youth as resources	Young people are given useful roles in the community.
	9. Service to others	Young person serves in the community one hour or more per week.
	10. Safety	Young person feels safe at home, school, and in the neighborhood.
Boundaries and Expectations	11. Family boundaries	Family has clear rules and consequences and monitors the young person's whereabouts.
	12. School boundaries	School provides clear rules and consequences.
	13. Neighborhood boundaries	Neighbors take responsibility for monitoring young people's behavior.
	14. Adult role models	Parent(s) and other adults model positive, responsible behavior.
	15. Positive peer influence	Young person's best friends model responsible behavior.
	16. High expectations	Both parent(s) and teachers encourage the young person to do well.
Constructive Use of Time	17. Creative activities	Young person spends three or more hours per week in lessons or practice in music, theater, or other arts.

	CATEGORY	ASSET NAME AND DEFINITION	
EXTERNAL ASSETS		18. Youth programs	Young person spends three or more hours per week in sports, clubs, or organizations at school and/or in community organizations.
		19. Religious community	Young person spends one hour or more per week in activities in a religious institution.
		20. Time at home	Young person is out with friends "with nothing special to do" two or fewer nights per week.
INTERNAL ASSETS	**Commitment to Learning**	21. Achievement motivation	Young person is motivated to do well in school.
		22. School engagement	Young person is actively engaged in learning.
		23. Homework	Young person reports doing at least one hour of homework every school day.
		24. Bonding to school	Young person cares about her or his school.
		25. Reading for pleasure	Young person reads for pleasure three or more hours per week.
	Positive Values	26. Caring	Young person places high value on helping other people.
		27. Equality and social justice	Young person places high value on promoting equality and reducing hunger and poverty.
		28. Integrity	Young person acts on convictions and stands up for her or his beliefs.

(continued)

CATEGORY	ASSET NAME AND DEFINITION	
INTERNAL ASSETS	29. Honesty	Young person "tells the truth even when it is not easy."
	30. Responsibility	Young person accepts and takes personal responsibility.
	31. Restraint	Young person believes it is important not to be sexually active or to use alcohol or other drugs.
Social Competencies	32. Planning and decision-making	Young person knows how to plan ahead and make choices.
	33. Interpersonal competence	Young person has empathy, sensitivity, and friendship skills.
	34. Cultural competence	Young person has knowledge of and comfort with people of different cultural/racial/ethnic backgrounds.
	35. Resistance skills	Young person can resist negative peer pressure and dangerous situations.
	36. Peaceful conflict resolution	Young person seeks to resolve conflict nonviolently.
Positive Identity	37. Personal power	Young person feels he or she has control over "things that happen to me."
	38. Self-esteem	Young person reports having a high self-esteem.
	39. Sense of purpose	Young person reports that "my life has a purpose."
	40. Positive view of personal future	Young person is optimistic about her or his personal future.

Young Adult Services Trainers Offer Their Services to School and Public Libraries

Are you looking for professional development or continuing education activities for your library staff? Do you need presenters at your state conference? Are you planning a workshop? If the answer is yes to any or all of these questions, you may want to contact one of the YALSA members listed below who have been trained to help school and public library staff members provide quality service to young adults.

YALSA has offered the services of this cadre of trainers since 1994. They were trained in three seminars offered by YALSA as a part of the Serving the Underserved: Customer Services for Young Adults project and have come to be known as the SUS trainers. As of June 2001, the total number of library staff members who have been trained is 14,376. They have been trained in a variety of settings, including school and public libraries and in state, regional and national conferences. The subjects they have covered include adolescent development, reading interests, behavioral problems, youth participation, facilities, and computer services for teens. The trainers have been trained to work with adult learners and are experts in the specialized field of library service to young adults.

The trainers keep in touch on YA-Train, their own private electronic list, and meet for dinner at each of the ALA conferences.

The names of the trainers presently active, their phone numbers and e-mail addresses, can be found at http://www.ala.org/yalsa/professional/trainersmain. html. If you are interested in a training session, please contact the trainers directly. You can discuss your ideas for a training session with as many of them as you like until you find the right fit. Each trainer handles his or her own arrangements for presentations.

If you have questions about the YALSA SUS training program, please contact the YALSA office at 1-800-545-2433 x 4390 or via e-mail at yalsa@ala.org.

Strategic Plan of the Young Adult Library Services Association

INTRODUCTION

The American Library Association (ALA) seeks to forge unity of purpose across divisions to guide them through changing times as well as to establish libraries and the library profession as essential to the intellectual life of all Americans.

To this end, the Young Adult Library Services Association (YALSA), a division of ALA, began a strategic planning process in 1996. Using ALA Goal 2000 as a guide, an environmental scan, and input from our membership and key stakeholders, we defined our unique mission, values, and vision. These elements and their resulting action steps became our strategic plan, which was adopted by the YALSA Board of Directors in June 1997. The plan's key concepts of advocacy, coalitions, and equity of access (ACE) have been YALSA's guiding principles, directing our comprehensive plan of action for the past four years.

Inspired by ALAction 2005, YALSA returned to its members and stakeholders to refocus its vision and purpose. The following plan is the result of this reexamination of YALSA's capacity and potential. The plan both mirrors and embraces the Key Action Areas of ALAction 2005 yet reflects our unique mission, "to advocate, promote and strengthen service to young adults."

Although YALSA is committed to this course of action, we will continue to review and update our plan yearly to ensure its relevancy.

Reprinted from YALSA Handbook Documents and Forms at www.ala.org/yalsa/yalsaintro/index.html

MISSION

The mission of YALSA is to advocate, promote, and strengthen service to young adults (ages 12-18) as part of the continuum of total library service, and to support those who provide library service to this population.

VISION

In every library in the nation, quality library service to young adults is provided by a staff that understands and respects the unique informational, educational, and recreational needs of young adults.

To ensure that this vision becomes a reality, the Young Adult Library Services Association (YALSA), a division of the American Library Association (ALA):

- advocates extensive and developmentally appropriate library and information services for young adults, ages 12 to 18;
- promotes reading and supports the literacy movement;
- advocates the use of information and communications technologies to provide effective library service;
- supports equality of access to the full range of library materials and services, including existing and emerging information and communications technologies, for young adults;
- provides education and professional development to enable its members to serve as effective advocates for young people;
- fosters collaboration and partnerships among its individual members with the library community and other groups involved in providing library and information services to young adults;
- influences public policy by demonstrating the importance of providing library and information services that meet the unique needs and interests of young adults;
- encourages research and is in the vanguard of new thinking concerning the provision of library and information services for youth;
- assures the intellectual freedom rights of young adults are supported and addressed through the actions of the division.

(Adopted June 1994)

VALUES

YALSA's values are related to its vision:

- Equal access to information, services and materials is recognized as a right, not a privilege for young adults.

- Young adults are actively involved in the library decision-making process.
- The library staff collaborates and cooperates with teachers, administrators, and workers in other youth-serving agencies to provide a holistic, community-wide network of activities and services that support healthy youth development.

KEY STRATEGIES

YALSA key strategies parallel and complement ALAction 2005, with a focus particular to the needs of young adults. While ALA focuses broadly on intellectual participation by all, YALSA's focus is on intellectual participation by young adults.

- Promote clearly and strongly YALSA's mission and vision to our professional colleagues and key partners to increase support for library service to young adults and positive youth development.
- Exploit technology for program support, management, member involvement, resource development, education, and shared learning.
- Expand resources and impact through networking, funding partnerships, and membership initiatives.
- Empower youth to participate in YALSA and in libraries.
- Form task forces to implement key action areas.

KEY PARTNERS

- Teenagers
- Media (websites, magazines, television, newspapers, etc.)
- Professional colleagues
- Educators
- Youth development organizations
- Parents
- Sponsors and partners of YALSA initiatives
- Government agencies
- Publishers
- Other divisions, units, and offices of the (ALA)

KEY ACTION AREAS

The key action areas have been placed in two tiers to stress the priority in which they should be addressed. The first tier contains the first three key action areas:

Advocacy, Education and Continuous Learning, and Coalitions. The second tier contains the last three key action areas: Literacy, Diversity, and Equity of Access.

Key Action Area I
Advocacy

A strong focus on advocacy is vital to the YALSA vision and its mission as the voice for library services for young adults. YALSA must widen its circles of influence advocating for young adults within our profession, our organization, and with other youth-serving organizations.

Strategies	Time line	Responsibility
Attach YALSA to ALA advocacy initiatives	Year 1	Staff/Executive Committee
Create a marketing initiative	Year 1	Staff/Executive Committee
Create an initiative to increase, maintain, and engage a diverse membership	Year 2	Cultural Diversity Task Force
Activities	Time line	Responsibility
Use the "@your library" logo and campaign at every possible opportunity	Years 1-3	Staff
Identify the elements of a YALSA marketing plan	Year 1	Executive Committee
Create a bookmark to promote YALSA	Year 2	Staff
Develop an advocacy brochure to explain and promote youth advocacy	Year 3	

Key Action Area II
Education and Continuous Learning

Continuing education and leadership development for YALSA membership is a critical course of action in a rapidly changing environment.

Strategies	Time line	Responsibility
Provide formal and informal learning communities and create training/mentoring opportunities for a strong, diverse membership	Year 1	Professional Development Committee
Bring YALSA's programs to state, local, and regional levels as well as to individual members	Year 2	Staff/SUS Trainers
Identify and collaborate with key partners to train young adults as community service providers and leaders	Year 3	Partnerships Advocating for Teens (PAT) Committee
Develop a plan to offer leadership training at conferences or institutes	Year 2	Youth Participation Committee
Activities	Time line	Responsibility
Appoint mentors for new members	Year 2	Division/Membership Promotional Committee
Present YALSA Institute at the AASL National Conference in November, 2001	Year 1	Institute Task Force
Initiate proposal to state agencies to bring SUS trainers to their states using LSTA grants	Year 1	Staff
Appoint a task force charged with developing proposals for leadership training	Year 2	Executive Committee
Develop web CE courses	Year 2	Staff/Professional Development Committee

Key Action Area III
Coalitions

Successful coalition building will broaden support for library service to young adults and expand resources.

Strategies	Time line	Responsibility
Evaluate our relationship to our key partners focusing on what our relationship to them should be and then:		
strengthen existing relationships	Year 1	PAT Committee
create new relationships	Year 2	PAT Committee
establish an effective presence within all relationships	Year 3	PAT Committee

Activities	Time line	Responsibility
Establish links to the websites of key partners identified by the PAT Committee	Year 1	PAT Committee
Seek sponsorships for Teen Read Week	Year 1	Staff
Ensure awareness of key partners to members who may wish to connect with them at the local level	Year 2	PAT Committee
Send YALSA representatives to key partners' meetings and conferences	Year 3	Executive Committee

Key Action Area IV
21st-Century Literacy

YALSA assists and promotes libraries in helping young adults develop the skills they need to seek and effectively utilize information resources.

Strategies	Time line	Responsibility
Define our role in literacy	Year 2	Literacy Task Force
Develop and implement a plan for literacy involvement	Year 2	Literacy Task Force

(continued)

Strategies	Time line	Responsibility
Select key partners in literacy education	Year 2	Literacy Task Force

Activities	Time line	Responsibility
Review ALAction Document #1: 21st Century Literacy	Year 2	Literacy Task Force
Research the meaning of literacy and create a definition unique to YALSA	Year 2	Literacy Task Force
Identify literacy elements in YALSA's programs and publications	Year 2	Literacy Task Force
Create a YALSA literacy action plan	Year 3	Literacy Task Force

Key Action Area V
Diversity

Library service to young adults focuses on individuals, and celebrates diversity. This focus is a fundamental value of YALSA and its members. Diversity is represented in the collection and services that libraries provide to young adults.

Strategies	Time line	Responsibility
Continue to develop and maintain diversity through YALSA lists of recommended resources, and YALSA programs and services	Years 1-3	Selection Committees
Develop a plan to attract and promote diversity in our membership	Year 2	

Activities	Time line	Responsibility
Actively support and encourage member participation in the Spectrum Initiative	Year 1	Board of Directors

Activities	Time line	Responsibility
Provide memberships for Spectrum scholars	Year 2	Board of Directors
Address diversity in a tip sheet and bibliography specifically for young adults	Year 2	Cultural Diversity Task Force
Prepare multicultural/multilingual lists of recommended resources	Year 3	Cultural Diversity Task Force
Work with the Spectrum initiative and integrate YALSA diversity needs with that initiative	Year 2	Cultural Diversity Task Force

Key Action Area VI
Equity of Access

Access issues are clearly articulated within ALA through the ALA Bill of Rights and other policy statements. Programs designed to expand access should reflect the full range of information resources, the diversity of the young adult population, and the interests of its members, with special attention to at-risk youth.

Strategies	Time line	Responsibility
Train members, partners, and young adults to be advocates for equity of access	Year 2	Professional Development Committee
Develop strategies to encourage appropriate allocation of resources to ensure equity of access	Year 2	Legislation Committee
Activities	**Time line**	**Responsibility**
Plan a program or web CE course that will train members to train young adults to be advocates for equity of access	Year 2	Intellectual Freedom Committee; Professional Development Committee
Use Teen Read Week as a vehicle for promoting equity of access in the provision of resources in libraries	Year 3	Teen Read Week Task Force/Staff

Association Outlook Environmental Scan

ASSOCIATION STRENGTHS

- High level of member participation and opportunities for involvement
- High level of member loyalty and commitment
- Members support and defend the rights of young adults including equal access and intellectual freedom
- Members provide powerful support to each other through collaboration and networking
- Leadership works as a team
- History of openness to change and experimentation
- Diversity of members in leadership roles
- Belief in youth participation in libraries
- National network of Serving the Underserved trainers
- Body of knowledge; expertise
- Emphasis on books and recommended book lists
- Focus on collaboration with other youth-serving organizations
- Focus on advocacy
- Focus on equality of access
- Major literacy initiative—Teen Read Week
- Growing membership
- Closer to financial security
- Growing market for products and services
- Broad representation of member roles

ASSOCIATION WEAKNESSES

- Membership is aging
- Revenues do not cover expenses
- Division needs subsidy from ALA and shared staffing agreement to survive
- Perceptions regarding "subsidized" division marginalizes perceived value to ALA
- Not enough resources for all good ideas
- Overlap with other types of services and types of library divisions
- Emphasis on books and recommended book lists

- Lack of commitment within the profession to the importance of quality services to young adults
- Lack of marketing services for division
- Not enough emphasis on diversity
- Current committee structure not flexible
- Lack of research on effectiveness of the book lists in the literacy movement
- Staff too small
- Too few CE opportunities
- Fee vs. free issues
- More resources needed to fully develop Teen Read Week into a major national initiative
- Not enough coordination with Washington office to take advantage of grant opportunities
- Lack of ethnic diversity in leadership

ENVIRONMENTAL OPPORTUNITIES

- Climate is ripe for emphasis on collaborative youth development, education and participation
- Global opportunities to serve teens
- Black, Asian and Pacific Islander, American Indian, Eskimo and Aleut, and Hispanic populations will make up an increasing share of the US population
- The nation can expect 1.3 million additional high school students by 2009
- Focus shifting from particular problems, e.g., drugs, pregnancy, etc., to coordination among agencies to provide healthy youth development activities (more comprehensive opportunities)
- Youth community services will be under one umbrella
- Greater emphasis and interest in after-school programs for youth
- The internet offers opportunities for global involvement

ENVIRONMENTAL CHALLENGES

- Lack of visibility and awareness of the work of young adult specialists
- Lack of uniform acceptance of services to young adults across the spectrum of various types of libraries
- Libraries not perceived by funders as important for youth development and education

- Low visibility with other youth-serving organizations
- Lack of leadership skills needed to be effective youth advocates
- Unwillingness of public and private school librarians to coordinate efforts to help youth become information literate
- Lack of training/career opportunities for YA specialists
- Lack of YA specialist positions in many public libraries
- There will be a growing shortage of school library media specialists and young adult specialists
- Not enough facilities or workforce to meet demand in schools and public libraries
- Access issues threaten equal rights for teens

RECOMMENDED POLICIES FOR IMPLEMENTATION

The Association's Strategic Plan was developed to be an essential ingredient in assuring the long term viability of YALSA. The plan was developed to assist YALSA in positioning for the future and maintaining its leadership in the field. It is, therefore, most important that the plan be fully integrated into the operational structure of YALSA. To make certain that the plan is utilized to the fullest possible extent, the following policies have been created.

Policy #1
Integration with the Association's programs, services, products

It shall be the policy of the YALSA Board of Directors that:

YALSA's Strategic Plan shall be provided to all parts of the association (standing committees, task forces, membership, partners, etc.) so that the goals and strategic directions contained in the plan may be used by these groups as they execute the work of the association. The plan shall be the primary basis for all YALSA programs, services and products, and these shall be evaluated on the basis of their relatedness to the plan.

The YALSA leadership shall be made aware of and be familiar with the YALSA Strategic Plan. The strategic directions from the plan shall be included on the agenda of each Midwinter planning session for discussion and comment. Recommendations for revisions to the plan will be solicited from throughout the association.

Policy #2
The Strategic Plan and priorities shall drive the budget process

It is recommended to the YALSA Board of Directors that:

The goals and strategic directions contained in the YALSA Strategic Plan shall provide the basis upon which the Board of Directors evaluate current programs, identify new initiatives, and establish priorities for the annual budget.

Policy #3
Assessment of implementation of the plan

It is recommended to the YALSA Board of Directors that:

Annually all committees and ad hoc groups identify programs and activities that support the plan for the current year and the two years that follow as well as those programs or activities that are no longer relevant. This information should be submitted annually to the YALSA office as part of the committee chair reporting process.

ANNUAL STRATEGIC PLAN UPDATING

It is recommended to the YALSA Board of Directors that:

The YALSA Strategic Plan is a living document that provides a framework for Association decision-making, programming, budgeting, and internal evaluation. Because YALSA operates within the rapidly evolving youth development environment, it is important for the document to be able to respond positively—even aggressively—as changes occur. Changes in the plan, however, must balance longer term objectives against more immediate issues.

Therefore, the Plan's strategic directions will be reviewed for change annually. YALSA units wishing consideration for particular changes in the strategic directions should submit their recommendations in writing to the Board 30 days prior to the Midwinter Meeting. Any action by the board will be following the planning session at the Midwinter Meeting.

In addition, each year a review of the association's external and internal environment shall be conducted by staff analyzing trends, member expectations and other available data. Based on this annual review, the Board of Directors may make other revisions to strategic directives and report these to the membership.

The vision, mission, goal statements, values and essential functions will be revisited by the board every five years at the Midwinter Meeting. The process for revision of the Strategic Plan will be ongoing. The more in-depth review will always follow active solicitation of input from both individual members and the various units of YALSA.*

---

* The Annual Strategic Plan Updating and Recommended Policies for Implementation sections are adapted from policies of the Association of College and Research Libraries (ACRL), a division of the American Library Association.

Normal Adolescent Development

from the American Academy of Child and Adolescent Psychology

Each teenager is an individual with a unique personality and special interests, likes and dislikes. In general, however, there is a series of developmental tasks that everyone faces during the adolescent years. A teenager's development can be divided into three stages—early, middle, and late adolescence. The normal feelings and behaviors of adolescents for each stage are described.

EARLY ADOLESCENCE (12-14 YEARS)

Movement towards Independence

Struggle with sense of identity

Moodiness

Improved abilities to use speech to express oneself

More likely to express feelings by action than by words

Close friendships gain importance

Less attention shown to parents, with occasional rudeness

Realization that parents are not perfect; identification of their faults

Search for new people to love in addition to parents

Tendency to return to childish behavior, fought off by excessive activity

Peer group influences interests and clothing styles

Career Interests

Mostly interested in present and near future

Greater ability to work

Sexuality

Girls ahead of boys

Same-sex friends and group activities

Shyness, blushing, and modesty

Show-off qualities

Greater interest in privacy

Experimentation with body (masturbation)

Worries about being normal

Ethics and Self-Direction

Rule and limit testing

Occasional experimentation with cigarettes, marijuana, and alcohol

Capacity for abstract thought

MIDDLE ADOLESCENCE

Movement towards Independence

Self-involvement, alternating between unrealistically high expectations and poor
self-concept

Complaints that parents interfere with independence

Extremely concerned with appearance and with one's own body

Feelings of strangeness about one's self and body

Lowered opinion of parents, withdrawal of emotions from them

Effort to make new friends

Strong emphasis on the new peer group with the group identity of selectivity,
superiority, and competitiveness

Periods of sadness as the psychological loss of the parents takes place

Examination of inner experiences, which may include writing a diary

Career Interests

Intellectual interests gain importance

Some sexual and aggressive energies directed into creative and career interests

Sexuality

Concerns about sexual attractiveness

Frequently changing relationships

Movement towards heterosexuality with fears of homosexuality

Tenderness and fears shown towards opposite sex

Feelings of love and passion

Ethics and Self-Description

Development of ideals and selection of role models

More consistent evidence of conscience

Greater capacity for setting goals

Interest in moral reasoning

LATE ADOLESCENCE (17-19 YEARS)

Movement towards Independence

Firmer identity

Ability to delay gratification

Ability to think ideas through

Ability to express ideas in words

More developed sense of humor

Stable interests

Greater emotional stability

Ability to make independent decisions

Ability to compromise

Pride in one's work

Self-reliance

Greater concern for others

Career Interests

More defined work habits

Higher level of concern for the future

Thoughts about one's role in life

Sexuality

Concerned with serious relationships

Clear sexual identity

Capacities for tender and sensual love

Ethics and Self-Direction

Capable of useful insight

Stress on personal dignity and self-esteem

Ability to set goals and follow through

Acceptance of social institutions and cultural traditions

Self-regulation of self-esteem

Toward a Blueprint for Youth: Making Positive Youth Development a National Priority

A collaboration to promote and support young people as resources and leaders for our communities and country

This statement of principles for the positive development of America's youth reflects the combined thoughts and support of youth-serving program officials in a broad range of federal departments, nonprofit organizations, advocacy organizations, intergovernmental associations and others, many of whom collaborated directly on this document (a complete list of supporting organizations is at the end).

WHAT IS POSITIVE YOUTH DEVELOPMENT?

Positive youth development is an approach toward all youth that builds on their assets and their potential and helps counter the problems that may affect them. Growing up can be tough for everyone, but young people are far more likely to succeed if they are active participants in decision-making that affects their lives and their communities.

Key elements of positive youth development are:

• Providing youth with safe and supportive environments.

Published by U.S. Department of Health and Human Services, Administration for Children and Families, Family and Youth Services Bureau. For more information about youth and positive youth development, go to the following web site: http://www.acf. dhhs.gov/programs/fysb/youthinfo.

- Fostering relationships between young people and caring adults who can mentor and guide them.
- Providing youth with opportunities to pursue their interests and focus on their strengths.
- Supporting the development of youths' knowledge and skills in a variety of ways, including study, tutoring, sports, the arts, vocational education, and service-learning.
- Engaging youth as active partners and leaders who can help move communities forward.
- Providing opportunities for youth to show that they care—about others and about society.
- Promoting healthy lifestyles and teaching positive patterns of social interaction.
- Providing a safety net in times of need.

THE TIME IS RIGHT

Today's young people are living in an exciting time, with an increasingly diverse society, new technologies, and expanding opportunities. To help ensure that they are prepared to become the next generation of parents, workers, leaders, and citizens, government agencies, national youth-serving organizations, foundations, and the business community are working together with a shared vision for the youth of our Nation:

> Every young person's contributions will be valued today, and he or she will grow up with the hope, opportunity and support needed for successful adulthood.

No one sector, acting alone, can ensure that all young people acquire the competencies, character, and protection they need to seize the opportunities that lie ahead. The time is right to make youth development a national priority, and the organizations that helped develop this publication pledge to do their part. They are committed to working together to:

- Spread the message within their own work and throughout the country that young people are resources and assets in our communities;
- Make their existing youth development efforts more well-known and accessible;
- Explore ways to provide more positive youth development opportunities; and
- Invest in our Nation's most important resource: our young people.

HOW POSITIVE YOUTH DEVELOPMENT MAKES A DIFFERENCE

Reflections from Young People

"The program helped me with the toughest issue—knowing who I am and what I am."

"You brought out the best in me when I didn't know there was a best. So now when I imagine how big is my future, I know it's as large as your love."

"I realize now that the program did not just offer me services and funds; it offered me a life."

"I am proud to say that I will be returning to school in the fall to finish my high school education. I'm not saying I don't make mistakes, but it's good to know that I have support when I do."

"If it wasn't for you guys, I wouldn't be here right now."

WHY SHOULD I SUPPORT POSITIVE YOUTH DEVELOPMENT?

- Positive youth development helps young people become independent and engaged citizens.
- Young people add tremendous value to dialogues on various issues in the community, offering different perspectives and new ideas.
- Research is beginning to show that the brain undergoes change during adolescence and may be affected, both positively and negatively, by experiences.
- Positive youth development encourages resilience, focusing on youths' strengths to overcome challenging situations.
- Positive youth development helps young people resist negative influences.
- Positive youth development programs can provide prevention services that reach youth identified as at risk in particular communities and that can serve to reduce the incidence of behaviors such as teen pregnancy, drug and alcohol use, dropping out of school, delinquency, and youth violence.
- Providing opportunities for young people to become independent is a good investment, avoiding potential problems that could be expensive to deal with later.
- Young people are future decision-makers and will become the leaders of our communities.

HOW CAN I SUPPORT POSITIVE YOUTH DEVELOPMENT?

- Encourage and assist all children and youth to focus on educational and developmental opportunities leading to lifelong learning. (Educational opportunities include guiding young people to master reading in the early grades; math in middle school; and rigorous courses in high school which prepare them for college, other post-secondary education, and employment. Developmental opportunities include a progressive series of activities and experiences that build cognitive skills and help young people become socially, morally, emotionally, and physically competent.)

- Work with community-based organizations and schools to build a seamless web of support, services, and opportunities that are culturally sensitive and address the full range of youth needs.

- Engage youth as full partners in community building, including active roles on boards and in program design, implementation, and evaluation.

- Encourage public awareness about the positive contributions of youth within communities.

- Engage local businesses to establish mentoring programs, apprenticeships, job training and employment opportunities for youth.

- Spread the word about positive youth development.

PROMOTING POSITIVE YOUTH DEVELOPMENT: SOME EXAMPLES

Safe Schools/Healthy Students Initiative: This unprecedented joint effort among the U.S. Departments of Education, Justice, Labor, and Health and Human Services helps communities design comprehensive educational, mental health, social, and juvenile justice services for youth. The services help young people develop the social skills and resilience necessary to avoid risky behaviors.

Girl Power!: This national public education campaign is sponsored by the Department of Health and Human Services and helps encourage and empower 9- to 14-year-old girls to make the most of their lives, providing positive messages, accurate health information, and support for girls and those who care about them.

21st-Century Community Learning Centers: The U.S. Department of Education and the Charles Stewart Mott Foundation have entered into a partnership to keep inner city and rural public schools open after regular school hours for enhanced learning and developmental opportunities. Schools, members of the National Collaboration for Youth, and other community-based organizations work together on this initiative.

4-H Clubs: Sponsored by the U.S. Department of Agriculture through the Cooperative Extension System, since 1902 the 4-H Clubs have offered activities and opportunities for growth, learning, and community involvement to youth in every county of the nation.

Youth Opportunity Movement: Sponsored by the U.S. Department of Labor, the vision is to ensure that all youth acquire the necessary skills and work experience to successfully transition into adulthood.

National Youth Network and National Organizations for Youth Safety: With support from the U.S. Departments of Justice and Transportation, these groups give youth an active role in the formulation of policies affecting them.

AmeriCorps: Of the more than 40,000 AmeriCorps members, most are young and in organizations focused on serving youth or engaging young people themselves to serve others. A special partnership between the Corporation for National Service and America's Promise supports 500 AmeriCorps Promise Fellows to give leadership to the Promise campaign in communities across the country.

Neighborhood Networks: This project of the Department of Housing and Urban Development provides nearly 1,000 multi-service computer technology community learning centers in public and low-income housing nationwide to teach computer literacy for 21st-century careers.

Child Care and Development Fund (CCDF): Nationwide, 35 percent of children receiving child-care subsidies through the CCDF are school-aged. This program, funded by the U.S. Department of Health and Human Services, also supports quality improvement activities such as professional development initiatives for staff in after-school programs.

ORGANIZATIONS ENDORSING THESE PRINCIPLES

America's Promise—The Alliance for Youth

Casey Family Programs
William T. Grant Foundation
W. K. Kellogg Foundation
David and Lucile Packard Foundation
Council of State Governments
National League of Cities
U.S. Conference of Mayors

IYF—US, International Youth Foundation

National Alliance of Business
National Campaign to Prevent Teen Pregnancy
National Collaboration for Youth including the:

Alliance for Children and Families
American Camping Association
American Red Cross
Association of Junior Leagues International
Big Brothers Big Sisters of America

Boy Scouts of America
Boys & Girls Clubs of America
Camp Fire USA (formerly Camp
  Fire Boys and Girls)
Campaign for Tobacco-Free Kids
Child Welfare League of America
Citizens' Scholarship Foundation
  of America
Coalition for Juvenile Justice
Communities in Schools
Families, 4-H and Nutrition
Girl Scouts of the USA
Girls Incorporated
Hostelling International—
  American Youth Hostels
Joint Action in Community
  Service
National Alliance for Hispanic
  Health
National Crime Prevention
  Council
National 4-H Council
National Mental Health
  Association
The National Mentoring
  Partnership
National Network for Youth
National Urban League
The Salvation Army
Save the Children

United Way of America
Volunteers of America
WAVE, Inc.
Women in Community Service
YMCA of the USA
Youth Law Center
YWCA of the USA
National Organizations for Youth
  Safety
National Training Institute for
  Community Youth Work
Search Institute
Young Adult Library Services
  Association
YouthBuild USA
Youth Service America

Corporation for National Service
U.S. Department of Agriculture
U.S. Department of Education
U.S. Department of Health and
  Human Services
U.S. Department of Housing and
  Urban Development
U.S. Department of Justice
U.S. Department of Labor
U.S. Department of Transportation

Guidelines for
Youth Participation

DEFINITION

Involvement of young adults, ages 12 through 18, in responsible action and significant services for their peers and the community.

INTRODUCTION

Although the concept of youth participation is neither foreign nor new, the Young Adult Library Services Association (YALSA) recognizes the need for a framework to facilitate the process of having young adults, ages 12 through 18, participate in any American Library Association activities at the national level.

Each committee or program chair is responsible for assessing the potential for the involvement of young adults, setting parameters for participation that specify objectives and outcomes and providing a balance between committee and young adult input. Neither committee decisions nor program content will be made based solely on young adult input but through a combination of professional knowledge and youth participation.

PURPOSE

To solicit the input of young adults and promote their participation in the creation and development of library activities, programs and publications, thus insuring the relevance of these products and services to the population we serve.

From the YALSA *Handbook of Organization,* approved by the YALSA Board of Directors, July 1997, revised June 2001

GOALS

- To organize and implement youth participation to support division and committee goals,
- To collect a wide range of ideas from as diverse a young adult population as possible,
- To create valuable experiences for the participating young adults in which they can gain knowledge and/or skills useful in future endeavors,
- To find opportunities for collaboration with other organizations that foster youth leadership.

PROCEDURES

Conference participation:

Identification of youth participation groups near conference sites: The Youth Participation Coordinator will make available to any ALA committee a list of local contacts six months prior to the event. Committees and programs are urged to draw from more than one group and to seek diverse input.

Requests to attend: Invitations to attend a committee meeting or participate in programs or other events will be extended by the committee chair.

Registration: Committee or program chairs should make name badges for young adults attending their programs, and send requests to the YALSA Office for guest exhibitor passes.

Conference expenses: Any expense relating to conference attendance is the responsibility of the youth participant, unless other arrangements have been approved by the division or unit.

Evaluation: As a part of the evaluation for programs and committee activities, chairs will assess the impact of youth participation in a report to the Youth Participation Coordinator.

POTENTIAL ACTIVITIES

- Creation of a YALSA teen advisory board
- Creation of an interactive Internet feature where teens can share ideas with each other and with librarians
- Training for youth as advocates for library services
- Development of materials to recruit for and inform about the library profession

- Observation of youth participation programs in conference city tours
- Involvement of local teens in planning and/or staffing exhibit booths
- Involvement of teens on the Local Arrangements Committee
- Involvement of teens in evaluating the market potential of library promotional materials
- Consideration of teens as presenters and participants in YALSA programs

The Nine Information Literacy Standards for Student Learning

from the American Association of School Librarians

INFORMATION LITERACY

Standard 1: The student who is information literate accesses information efficiently and effectively.

Standard 2: The student who is information literate evaluates information critically and competently.

Standard 3: The student who is information literate uses information accurately and creatively.

INDEPENDENT LEARNING

Standard 4: The student who is an independent learner is information literate and pursues information related to personal interests.

Standard 5: The student who is an independent learner is information literate and appreciates literature and other creative expressions of information.

Standard 6: The student who is an independent learner is information literate and strives for excellence in information seeking and knowledge generation.

Reproduced from *Information Literacy Standards for Student Learning* (AASL 1998), 8-9 (http://www.ala.org/AASL)

SOCIAL RESPONSIBILITY

Standard 7: The student who contributes positively to the learning community and to society is information literate and recognizes the importance of information to a democratic society.

Standard 8: The student who contributes positively to the learning community and to society is information literate and practices ethical behavior in regard to information and information technology.

Standard 9: The student who contributes positively to the learning community and to society is information literate and participates effectively in groups to pursue and generate information.

Excerpt from Adolescent Literacy: A Position Statement

1. Adolescents deserve access to a wide variety of reading material that they can and want to read.

The account of Kristy and Nick's day* shows adolescents reading inside- and outside-of-school print such as textbooks, paperbacks, magazines, and Web sites. Yet national assessments provoke concern about the amount of such reading among adolescents. For instance, the 1996 NAEP [National Assessment of Educational Progress] findings indicate that about one quarter of the tested adolescents reported daily reading of five or fewer pages in school and for homework. As students grow older, the amount of time they read for fun declines. About one half of the tested 9-year-old students reported reading for fun on a daily basis, whereas only about one quarter of the 17-year-old students reported doing so. Literacy research and professional judgment support at least four reasons for providing adolescents access to inside- and outside-of-school reading materials they can and want to read.

Time spent reading is related to reading success. If students devote some time every day reading connected text, their word knowledge, fluency, and comprehension tend to increase. Reading continuously for a brief part of each day is a small investment for a large return.

Time spent reading is associated with attitudes toward additional reading. Students who habitually read in the present tend to seek out new materials in the future. These students are on the way to lifelong reading.

---

*"Adolescent Literacy: A Position Statement" begins with a description of the role that reading plays in the lives of two typical adolescents—Kristy and Nick.

Reprinted with permission of the International Reading Association

Time spent reading is tied to knowledge of the world. Combining materials such as textbooks, library books, paperbacks, magazines, and Websites provides full accounts of phenomena, new vocabulary, and up-to-date information. These materials permit readers to expand and strengthen their grasp of the world.

Reading is a worthwhile life experience. Readers can find comfort and delight in print. Vicariously stepping into text worlds can nourish teens' emotions and psyches as well as their intellects. Providing opportunities to achieve the outcomes just listed is accomplished through a network of educators, librarians, parents, community members, peers, policy makers, technology providers, and publishers. These groups affect middle and high school students' access to wide reading by shaping the following elements:

Time. An often overlooked—yet essential—component of access to reading is the time available for it. Adolescents deserve specific opportunities to schedule reading into their days.

Choice. Choosing their own reading materials is important to adolescents who are seeking independence. All adolescents, and especially those who struggle with reading, deserve opportunities to select age-appropriate materials they can manage and topics and genres they prefer. Adolescents deserve classroom, school, and public libraries that offer reading materials tied to popular television and movie productions; magazines about specific interests such as sports, music, or cultural backgrounds; and books by favorite authors. They deserve book clubs, class sets of paperbacks, and personal subscriptions to magazines.

Support. Time and choice mean little if there is no support. Support includes actions such as bringing books to the classroom, arousing interest in them, orally reading selections, and fostering student-to-student and student-to-adult conversations about what is read. Adolescents deserve these supports so they will identify themselves as readers and take advantage of the times and choices that are offered.

2. Adolescents deserve instruction that builds both the skill and desire to read increasingly complex materials.

Kristy and Nick Araujo tackled their assignments with a few basic reading and writing strategies. Outlining text passages and looking up an unfamiliar word like *dispel* in the dictionary are some of strategies Nick and Kristy used in their studies. However, these teens will need to expand their strategies to handle increasingly complex material now and in the future. In addition, Nick's history as a struggling reader indicates he will need extra help if he is to grasp future concepts successfully.

Adolescents need well-developed repertoires of reading comprehension and study strategies such as the following:

- questioning themselves about what they read;
- synthesizing information from various sources;
- identifying, understanding, and remembering key vocabulary;
- recognizing how a text is organized and using that organization as a tool for learning;
- organizing information in notes;
- interpreting diverse symbol systems in subjects such as biology and algebra;
- searching the Internet for information;
- judging their own understanding; and
- evaluating authors' ideas and perspectives.

Many teaching practices are available for supporting adolescent learners as they apply strategies to complex texts. For example, teachers who introduce some of the technical vocabulary students will encounter in a chapter help reduce comprehension problems, and students help themselves by independently previewing passages and discerning the meanings of unfamiliar words. Study-guide questions and statements that prompt students from literal understandings to higher order ones also foster comprehension. When teachers inform students while the guides are being phased out, adolescents can appropriate for themselves the thinking strategies the guides stimulated.

Middle and secondary schools where reading specialists work with content area teachers in the core areas of science, mathematics, English, and social studies show great promise. For example, a reading specialist's work with a social studies teacher to map ideas during a unit on the Aztec, Inca, and Mayan cultures can become the basis for teaching students to map ideas as an independent study strategy. The CAL recommends that content area teachers and reading specialists work together to effectively support adolescents' development of advanced reading strategies.

Developing students' advanced reading skills is insufficient if adolescents choose not to read. Unfortunately, students' attitudes toward reading tend to decline as they advance into the middle grades, with a particularly disturbing impact on struggling readers like Nick. Attitudes toward reading contribute to reading achievement.

Caring teachers who act on adolescents' interests and who design meaningful inquiry projects address motivational needs. For example, Kristy was excited about independently researching events of the Great Depression that affected Cassie's life in *Roll of Thunder, Hear My Cry*. Based on her experiences in this class, Kristy knew she would have an attentive audience for discussing her research and a considerate teacher supporting and evaluating her demonstration of knowledge. Mrs. Mangrum regularly fostered discussions of multicultural literature, and she expressed sincere interest in her students' wide ranging cultural and ethnic differences, learning styles, and needs for respect and security. In addition to having the whole class read and talk about one particular novel, Mrs. Mangrum provided students access to various books for self-selected reading on their own. She gleaned books from her own classroom collection, students' recommendations, and a close working relationship with her school librarian. Adolescents deserve classrooms like Mrs. Mangrum's that knowingly promote the desire to read.

3. Adolescents deserve assessment that shows them their strengths as well as their needs and that guides their teachers to design instruction that will best help them grow as readers.

National-level mandates on education such as Goals 2000 and the reauthorization of the Elementary and Secondary Education Act in the United States require that states develop standards for instruction and assess student achievement of the standards. In some states these measures are being used to determine the type of diploma students receive and whether or not students will even graduate. Although state assessments are useful in monitoring the achievement of standards, they rarely indicate specific teaching-learning experiences that foster literacy development.

Adolescents deserve classroom assessments that bridge the gap between what they know and are able to do and relevant curriculum standards; they deserve assessments that map a path toward continued literacy growth. For instance, when Nick began writing his essay about a famous person, he did not seem clear about the expected standards. He probably would have benefited from understanding how writing this particular essay connected with the world beyond the classroom. He could have used lessons on how to accomplish expectations. He might have benefited from examining papers that reflected the expected standards. And he could have profited from a rubric or scoring guide that clearly articulated the standards for evaluation.

Conferring with his teacher and classmates about how his efforts fit curriculum standards also might have promoted Nick's writing. During such conferences he would have opportunities to assess his own writing, set specific goals, and decide on strategies for achieving his goals. Further, Nick would benefit from maintaining a record of his efforts in something like a portfolio to help gauge his reading and writing growth and plan appropriate actions. Emphasizing relevance and self-improvement in classroom assessment encourages adolescents to invest themselves in learning. It helps them understand how to control the rate and quality of their own literacy growth.

Effective assessments are crucial for students who come from environments that differ from Kristy and Nick's. Using tests simply to determine which students will graduate or which type of diploma students will receive especially disadvantages adolescents from homes where English is not the first language or where poverty endures. It wrongs those most in need of enriched educational opportunities.

In sum, the CAL [Commission on Adolescent Literacy of the International Reading Association] believes that adolescents deserve classroom assessments that

- are regular extensions of instruction;
- provide usable feedback based on clear, attainable, and worthwhile standards;
- exemplify quality performances illustrating the standards; and
- position students as partners with teachers evaluating progress and setting goals.

4. Adolescents deserve expert teachers who model and provide explicit instruction in reading comprehension and study strategies across the curriculum.

Like masters with apprentices, expert teachers immerse students in a discipline and teach them how to control it. Expert teachers engage students with a novel such as *Roll of Thunder, Hear My Cry* in Kristy's language arts class or a topic such as the presentation of self in Nick's psychology class. Then they teach reading, writing, and thinking strategies that enable students to explore and learn about subject matter. Reading and subject matter teachers often collaborate to provide such instruction.

If Kristy's teacher, Mrs. Mangrum, were teaching self-questioning as a strategy, she might first take a chapter of *Roll of Thunder, Hear My Cry* and model queries such as "What became clear to me?" and "I wonder why Cassie didn't complain to her teacher about the school bus driver running them off the road." Mrs. Mangrum would explain how she arrived at answers to her questions, thinking through the process aloud. She would explicitly demonstrate how to ask and answer productive questions during this stage of instruction.

Next Mrs. Mangrum and Kristy's class might produce questions and answers collectively, again thinking aloud. At first they might stay with the chapter Mrs. Mangrum began with, or they might move to another. Together the students and teacher would explain and comment on what they were doing. Additionally, Mrs. Mangrum might provide written guides for students to question themselves, exploring and experimenting with the strategy on their own. She also might design small-group assignments that encourage students to reflect on self-questioning, sharing how they used it and difficulties they overcame.

Eventually Mrs. Mangrum would expect Kristy and her classmates to apply self-questioning on their own. She would remind students to question themselves while reading other novels and passages later in the year. Throughout this cycle of instruction, she would have students assess how well they were accomplishing the strategy.

Research on expert teachers has produced an image of decision makers effectively orchestrating classroom life. Expert teachers help students get to the next level of strategy development by addressing meaningful topics, making visible certain strategies, then gradually releasing responsibility for the strategies to the learners. Adolescents deserve such instruction in all their classes.

5. Adolescents deserve reading specialists who assist individual students having difficulty learning how to read.

In the early 1900s standardized tests in the United States revealed large numbers of adolescents reading well below expectations. This finding sparked many educators and members of the public to develop programs for adolescents that included remedial instruction in reading classes and modified instruction in regular subject-matter classes. Federally funded programs to compensate for the effects of poverty on achievement later were instituted for reading, writing, and mathematics instruction.

National-level data continue highlighting the presence of adolescents like Nick with reading needs. For instance, 13% of fall 1989 first-year higher education students in the United States were enrolled in courses devoted specifically to remedial reading. The high school dropout rate, which is related to literacy difficulties, was 11% in 1993. Race, ethnicity, and economic status continue to be strongly associated with reading achievement. Although the number of secondary schools that assist adolescents who struggle with reading is declining, most schools still provide programs. These include widely varying provisions such as special education classes, after-school tutoring, and content reading integration.

Reading difficulties do not occur in a vacuum. Adolescents' personal identities, academic achievement, and future aspirations mix with ongoing difficulties with reading. Because literacy promises to enhance individuals as well as society, adolescents struggling with reading deserve assistance by professionals specially prepared in reading. The CAL recommends services that include the following:

- providing tutorial reading instruction that is part of a comprehensive program connected with subject matter teachers, parents, and the community;
- structuring challenging, relevant situations in special reading classes and in subject matter classrooms where students succeed and become self-sufficient learners;
- assessing students' reading and writing—and enabling students to assess their own reading and writing—to plan instruction, foster individuals' control of their literacy, and immediately support learners when progress diminishes;
- teaching vocabulary, fluency, comprehension, and study strategies tailored to individuals' competencies;
- relating literacy practices to life management issues such as exploring careers, examining individuals' roles in society, setting goals, managing time and stress, and resolving conflicts; and

- offering reading programs that recognize potentially limiting forces such as work schedules, family responsibilities, and peer pressures.

6. Adolescents deserve teachers who understand the complexities of individual adolescent readers, respect their differences, and respond to their characteristics.

Adolescents demonstrate substantial differences. In the Araujo family, Nick's interests in film and the outdoors differed from Kristy's preferences for athletics and teen culture. Nick tended to struggle with and avoid school-based reading and writing tasks; Kristy generally excelled with and enthusiastically approached them.

Viewing members of one family in relation to another calls attention to additional differences. Factors such as family heritage, language, and social and economic position contribute to the variation that students regularly display during reading and writing activities.

Differences also are apparent when individuals are considered one at a time. Nick often was preoccupied in one class, English, but highly engaged in another, psychology. Kristy hated how her science teacher conducted class but enjoyed language arts. Nick and Kristy probably acted slightly differently from day to day in all their classes depending on what was happening in their personal worlds.

Adolescents deserve classrooms that respect individuals' differences. To promote respect, teachers encourage the exchange of ideas among individuals. They regularly set up paired, small-group, and whole-class arrangements so that everyone can have his or her voice heard. Believing that everyone has something to offer, they organize instruction so students of diverse backgrounds share their insights into course topics. One of the reasons Kristy eagerly researched the Great Depression was that she anticipated a productive discussion the next day.

Respectful classrooms are safe enough for students to take risks when expressing themselves publicly. No rudeness, put-downs, or ugly remarks are allowed. Learners address others courteously and expect courteous treatment in turn. They disagree without being disagreeable, contesting others' ideas without personal insults.

Respectful classrooms also display positive expectations. Teachers believe that students who are taught appropriately can meet rigorous standards. They acknowledge conditions outside of class that might interfere with learning, but they inspire teens to be resilient and take charge of their lives. Learning failures are unacceptable.

Along with respect, individual adolescents deserve teachers who respond to their characteristics. Responsive teachers address the mandated curriculum while engaging students in self-expression. To illustrate, Nick's five-paragraph report on a famous person could be extended several ways. Nick could inquire into Davy Crockett through interviews, library materials, and textbooks as well as through the Internet. He could enrich his investigation by examining legendary aspects of

Crockett or he could look at Crockett's role as an icon of individualism. Nick could supplement his essay by representing Crockett through a poem, poster, Readers Theatre, or skit. Teachers often limit such choices to manageable options, but they offer choices and supports for accomplishing them.

In sum, adolescents deserve more than a centralized, one-size-fits-all approach to literacy. They deserve teachers who establish productive conditions for learning; move into individuals' worlds with respect, choice, and support; and move out to allow growth.

7. Adolescents deserve homes, communities, and a nation that will support their efforts to achieve advanced levels of literacy and provide the support necessary for them to succeed.

For adolescents, growing in literacy means being continually stretched. Because of this, adolescents deserve all the support they can get, not only from school but from their families, communities, and the nation.

Parents play an important role. They help adolescents extend and consolidate their literacy by engaging them in discussions about what they read, responding sincerely to the ideas they write, and making printed materials available. Parents become partners with educators in supporting their adolescents' growth.

Members of the local community often are partners with adolescents. Libraries, religious groups, and after-school programs are centers for community workers and volunteers to assist adolescents with homework, tutor individuals with learning difficulties, and initiate book discussion groups. Businesses become partners with schools by providing mentors and role models as well as funds for buying books and recognizing achievements.

Adolescents preparing for the 21st century deserve new forms of collaboration among educators. Community colleges, technical schools, and universities can offer input and assistance. Professional organizations working together and exploring relationships among reading, writing, and learning may lead to new educational directions. The educational community can demonstrate that adolescent literacy is important.

The many dimensions of adolescent literacy are addressed best in school reform and restructuring that place the growth of students at the center of every activity. Environments of high expectations, inquiry, and decision making encourage students to refine the reading and writing abilities they have and take the risks necessary to grow. Adolescents deserve new perspectives on what it means to know a subject and to display that knowledge. Surface changes to schools involving scheduling and required courses are not enough to fully support adolescents' advanced reading and writing.

Finally, the CAL believes that the literacy achievement of adolescents cannot grow to new levels without changes in governmental policy. Emphasizing the achievement of early readers has not produced adolescents who read and write at high levels of proficiency. Adolescents deserve increased levels of governmental support. This includes appropriate funding for intervention services in the upper grades, the point in most comparisons at which children in the United States perform less well. School libraries can be the center of efforts to encourage wide reading, but for decades they have seen a steady decline in funding. Governmental support also involves exerting leadership to mobilize initiatives among parents and local communities.

Government can support ongoing staff development for helping students grow in literacy as they grow in content knowledge. Furthermore, government can support literacy research concentrating on the upper grades where literacy proficiencies are less well understood than those at the lower grades.

Young Adults Deserve the Best: Competencies for Librarians Serving Young Adults

AREA I—LEADERSHIP AND PROFESSIONALISM

The librarian will be able to:

1. Develop and demonstrate leadership skills in articulating a program of excellence for young adults.

2. Exhibit planning and evaluating skills in the development of a comprehensive program for young adults.

3. Develop and demonstrate a commitment to professionalism.

   a. Adhere to the American Library Association Code of Ethics.

   b. Demonstrate a non-judgmental attitude toward young adults.

   c. Preserve confidentiality in interactions with young adults.

4. Plan for personal and professional growth and career development through active participation in professional associations and continuing education.

5. Develop and demonstrate a strong commitment to the right of young adults to have physical and intellectual access to information that is consistent with the American Library Association's Library Bill of Rights.

6. Demonstrate an understanding of and a respect for diversity in cultural and ethnic values.

7. Encourage young adults to become lifelong library users by helping them to discover what libraries have to offer and how to use libraries.

Reprinted from www.ala.org/yalsa/yalsainfo/competencies.html

AREA II—KNOWLEDGE OF CLIENT GROUP

The librarian will be able to:

1. Apply factual and interpretative information on adolescent psychology, growth and development, sociology, and popular culture in planning for materials, services and programs for young adults.
2. Apply knowledge of the reading process and of types of reading problems in the development of collections and programs for young adults.
3. Identify the special needs of discrete groups of young adults and design and implement programs and build collections appropriate to their needs.

AREA III—COMMUNICATION

The librarian will be able to:

1. Demonstrate effective interpersonal relations with young adults, administrators, other professionals who work with young adults, and the community at large by:
   a. Using principles of group dynamics and group process.
   b. Establishing regular channels of communication (both written and oral) with each group.
2. Apply principles of effective communication which reinforces positive behaviors in young adults.

AREA IV—ADMINISTRATION

A. Planning

The librarian will be able to:

1. Develop a strategic plan for library service to young adults.
   a. Formulate goals, objectives, and methods of evaluation for a young adult program based on determined needs.
   b. Design and conduct a community analysis and needs assessment.
   c. Apply research findings for the development and improvement of the young adult program.
   d. Design, conduct, and evaluate local action research for program improvement.
2. Design, implement, and evaluate an ongoing public relations and report program directed toward young adults, administrators, boards, staff, other agencies serving young adults, and the community at large.

3. Identify and cooperate with other information agencies in networking arrangements to expand access to information for young adults.
4. Develop, justify, administer, and evaluate a budget for the young adult program.
5. Develop physical facilities which contribute to the achievement of young adult program goals.

B. Managing

The librarian will be able to:

1. Supervise and evaluate other staff members who work with young adults.
2. Design, implement, and evaluate an ongoing program of professional development.
3. Develop policies and procedures for the efficient operation of all technical functions, including acquisition, processing, circulation, collection maintenance, equipment supervision, and scheduling of young adult programs.
4. Identify external sources of funding and other support and apply for those suitable for the young adult program.
5. Monitor legislation and judicial decisions pertinent to young adults, especially those that affect youth rights, and disseminate this information.

AREA V—KNOWLEDGE OF MATERIALS

The librarian will be able to:

1. Formulate collection development and selection policies for young adult materials, consistent with the parent institutions' policies.
2. Using a broad range of selection sources, develop a collection of materials for young adults that includes all appropriate formats.
3. Demonstrate a knowledge and appreciation of literature for young adults.
4. Identify current reading, viewing, and listening interests of young adults and incorporate these findings into collection development and programs.
5. Design and locally produce materials in a variety of formats to expand the collections.
6. Incorporate new and improved technology (e.g., computers and software, digitized information, video, the Internet and the World Wide Web) into young adult collections and programs.
7. Maintain awareness of ongoing technological advances and a minimum level of expertise with electronic resources.

AREA VI—ACCESS TO INFORMATION

The librarian will be able to:

1. Organize collections to guarantee easy and equitable access to information for young adults.
2. Use current standard methods of cataloging and classification, as well as incorporate the newest means of electronic access to information.
3. Create an environment which attracts and invites young adults to use the collection.
4. Develop special tools which provide access to information not readily available (e.g., community resources, special collections, and links to appropriate and useful websites).
5. Create and disseminate promotional materials that will ease access to collections and motivate their use.

AREA VII—SERVICES

The librarian will be able to:

1. Utilize a variety of techniques (e.g., booktalking, discussion groups) to encourage use of materials.
2. Provide a variety of information services (e.g., career information, homework help, websites) to meet the diverse needs of young adults.
3. Instruct young adults in the basic information gathering and research skills. These should include the skills necessary to use and evaluate electronic information sources, and to ensure current and future information literacy.
4. Encourage young adults in the use of all types of materials for their personal growth and enjoyment.
5. Design, implement, and evaluate specific programs and activities (both in the library and in the community) for young adults, based on their needs and interests.
6. Involve young adults in planning and implementing services and programs for their age group.

Approved by the Young Adult Library Services Association Board of Directors, June 1981. Revised January 1998.

RESOURCES CITED

Adolescent literacy: A position statement. 1999. *Journal of Adolescent and Adult Literacy* 44 (1): 97-110.

American Academy of Child and Adolescent Psychology. 1996. Normal adolescent development. Available [Online]: http://education.indiana.edu/cas/adol/development.html>. 6 July 2001.

American Association of School Librarians and Association for Educational Communications and Technology. 1998. *Information literacy standards for student learning.* Chicago: American Library Assn.

_____. 1998. *Information power: Building partnerships for learning.* Chicago: American Library Assn.

Aronson, Marc. 2002. Coming of age: One editor's view of how young adult publishing developed in America. *Publishers Weekly* (February 11): 82-86.

Benson, Peter. 1992. *The troubled journey: A profile of American youth.* Minneapolis, Minn.: Search Institute and Free Spirit.

_____. 1997. *All kids are our kids: What communities must do to raise caring and responsible children and adolescents.* San Francisco: Jossey-Bass.

_____. 1999. *A fragile foundation: The state of developmental assets among youth.* Minneapolis, Minn.: Search Institute.

Bottoms, Gene. 2001. High standards necessary to raise literacy levels of all students. Southern Regional Education Board press release. Available [Online]: <www.sreb.org/main/Publications/PressRel/news1.asp?Code-1055>. 7 January 2002.

Boyle, Peter. 2001. Scientists dissect youth development. *Youth Today* 10 (December/January): 38-40.

Commission on Adolescent Literacy. 1999. Adolescent literacy: A position statement. International Reading Association. Available [Online]: <www.ira.org/pdf/1036.pdf>. 20 April 2002.

Doyle, Christina. 1992. *Outcome measures for information literacy within the National Education Goal of 1990. Final report to National Forum on Information Literacy.* Syracuse, N.Y.: ERIC (ED351033).

Hersch, Patricia. 1998. *A tribe apart: A journey into the heart of American adolescence.* New York: Ballantine.

Hoff, David. 2001. U.S. students rank among world's best and worst readers. *Education Week* 21 (December 12): 7.

Lance, Keith Curry, Marcia Rodney, and Christine Hamilton-Pennell. 2000. *How school libraries help kids achieve standards: The second Colorado study.* Denver: Library Research Service. Available [Online]: <www.lrs.org/documents/imcstudies/CO/execsumm.pdf>. 10 February 2002.

Mediavilla, Cindy. 2001. *Creating the full-service homework center in your library.* Chicago: American Library Assn.

National Assessment of Education Progress (NAEP). 1999. Reading report card for the nations and states. National Center for Educational Statistics. Available [Online]: <http://nces.ed.gov/pubsearch/pubsinfo.asp?pubid=1999500>.

National Collaboration for Youth (NCY). 2001. A national youth development agenda: Public policy statements of the National Collaboration for Youth. Available [Online]: <www.nydic.org>. 8 October 2001.

National Education Association (NEA) poll on the reading habits of adolescents. 2001. Conducted by Peter D. Hart Research Associates from February 9 to 15, 2001. Available [Online]: <www.nea.org/readingmatters/readpoll.html>. 20 March 2001.

National Research Council and Institute of Medicine. 2001. *Community programs to promote youth development.* Committee on Community-Level Programs for Youth. Jacquelynne Eccles and Jennifer A. Gootman, eds. Board on Children, Youth and Families, Division of Behavioral and Social Sciences and Education. Washington, D.C.: National Academy Pr.

Nelson, Sandra. 2001. *The new planning for results: A streamlined approach.* Chicago: American Library Assn.

Neuman, Susan B., and Donna Celano. 2001. Access to print in low-income and middle-income communities: An ecological study of four neighborhoods. *Reading Research Quarterly* 36 (1): 8-26.

Pittman, Karen J. and Wanda E. Fleming. 1991. *A new vision: Promoting youth development.* Written transcript of live testimony by Karen J. Pittman given before the House Select Committee on Children, Youth and Families. Washington, D.C.: Center for Youth Development and Policy Research.

Rodger, Eleanor Jo. 1994. Public opinion about the roles of the public library in the community: The results of a recent Gallup poll. *Public Libraries* 33 (January/February): 23-28.

Sarlin, Peggy. 2001. Letter to the editor. *West Side Spirit* (October 18). Available [Online]: <www.stuypa.org>. 1 November 2001.

Search Institute. 1997. The forty developmental assets. Available [Online]: <www. search-institute.org/assetsforty.htm>.

_____. 1999. *A fragile foundation: The state of developmental assets among American youth* by Peter L. Benson, Peter C. Scales, and Eugene C. Roehlkepartain. Minneapolis, Minn.: Search Institute.

_____. 2000. Developmental assets: An overview. Available [Online]: <www.search-institute.org/assets>.

Sheppard, Beverly. 2001. *The Twenty-first-century learner.* Washington, D.C.: Institute of Museum and Library Services.

SmartGirl.org and Young Adult Library Services Association. 2001. Teen Read Week survey: Reading habits and respondent behavior and opinion. Available [Online]: <www.ala.org/teenread/trw_surveyresults.pdf>. April 2002.

Sullivan, Ed. 2001. Teenagers are not luggage: They don't need handling. *Public Libraries* 40 (2): 75-77.

U.S. Dept. of Commerce. 2000. *Falling through the net: Toward digital inclusion: A report on America's access to technology tools.* Washington, D.C.: Government Printing Office.

U.S. Dept. of Education. Office of Educational Research and Improvement. National Center for Education Statistics. 1995. *Services and resources for children and young adults in public libraries.* Washington, D.C.: Government Printing Office.

U.S. Dept. of Health and Human Services, Administration for Children and Families. 1999. Toward a blueprint for youth: Making positive youth development a national priority. Available [Online]: <www.acf.dhhs.gov/programs/fysb/youthinfo>. Washington, D.C.: Dept. of Health and Human Services.

Web-Based Education Commission. 2000. *The power of the Internet for learning: Moving from promise to practice.* Washington, D.C.: The Commission. Available [Online]: <www.ed.gov/offices/AC/WBEC/FinalReport>.

Whalen, Samuel P., Joan Costello, and Julie Spielberger, et al. 2001. *Connecting young adults to the transforming public library: A map to practice and policy.* Draft. Chicago: Chapin Hall Center for Children.

Young Adult Library Services Association. 2001. *Handbook of organization.* Chicago: Young Adult Library Services Association. Available [Online]: <www.ala.org/yalsa/yalsainfo/html>.

Young Adult Library Services Association and Public Library Association. 1993. *Bare bones: Young adult services tips for public library generalists* by Mary K. Chelton and James M. Rosinia in collaboration with the Public Library Association/Young Adult Library Services Association Interdivisional Committee on Young Adult Services in Public Libraries. Chicago: American Library Assn.

_____. 1993. *Directions for library service to young adults.* 2nd ed. Chicago: American Library Assn.

_____. 2000. *Bare bones young adult services: Tips for public library generalists* by Renée J. Vaillancourt. Public Library Association and Young Adult Library Services Association. Chicago: American Library Assn.

Young Adult Services Division of the American Library Association. 1977. *Directions for library service to young adults.* Chicago: American Library Assn.

RESOURCES FOR FURTHER READING

Adams, Deborah. 1999. Where no young adult services have gone before: The diary of a startup YA librarian. *Voice of Youth Advocates* 22: 68-71.

American Association of School Librarians. [n.d.] Position statement on the value of library media programs in education. Available [Online]: <www.ala.org/aasl/ positions/ps_value.html>.

_____. 1994. Information literacy: A position paper on information problem solving. Developed by the Wisconsin Educational Media Association and endorsed by the Wisconsin Department of Public Instruction. Adopted and formatted by the American Association of School Librarians with additional scenarios by Paula Montgomery. Bibliography revised 1999. Available [Online]: <www.ala. org/aasl/positions/ps.infolit.html>.

_____. 1999. *A planning guide for information power: Building partnerships for learning with school library media program assessment rubric for the twenty-first century.* Chicago: American Library Assn.

_____. 1999. Position statement on the value of independent reading in the school library media program. Available [Online]: <www.ala.org/aasl/positions/ps_ independent.html>. Adopted June 1994; revised July 1999.

_____. 2000. Access to resources and services in the school library media program: An interpretation of the Bill of Rights. Available [Online]: <www.ala. org/aasl/positions/ps_billofrights.html>.

American Library Association. 2000. *Recognizing excellence in afterschool programs for young adults*. (Brochure) Chicago: American Library Assn.

Anderson, Shelia, and James Bradford. 2001. State-level commitment to public library services to young adults. *Journal of Youth Services in Libraries* 14 (3): 23-27.

Aronson, Marc. 2001. *Exploding the myths: The truth about teens and reading*. Lanham, Md.: Scarecrow.

Beers, G. Kylene. 1996. No time, no interest, no way! The three voices of aliteracy. *School Library Journal* (February): 30-33.

_____. 1996. No time, no interest, no way! Part 2. *School Library Journal* (March): 110-113.

Begley, Sharon. 2000. A world of their own. *Newsweek* (May 8): 52-57.

Benson, Peter. 1998. *What teens need to succeed*. Minneapolis, Minn.: Free Spirit.

Benton Foundation. 1996. *Buildings, books, and bytes: Libraries and communities in the digital age*. Washington, D.C.: The Foundation.

_____. 1998. *Losing ground bit by bit: Low-income communities in the Information Age*. Washington, D.C.: National Urban League/Benton Foundation.

Bradburn, Frances Bryant. 1999. *Output measures for school library media programs*. New York: Neal-Schuman.

Broderick, Dorothy. 1995. Building the bridge to adult literacy. *Voice of Youth Advocates* 18 (April): 6.

Brownlee, Shannon. 1999. Inside the teen brain. *U.S. News & World Report* 127 (August 9): 44-48.

Byczek, Jane R., and Renée J. Vaillancourt. 1998. Lone ranger: YA librarians alone on the range. *Voice of Youth Advocates* 21: 105-108+.

Cannon, Angie. 2000. Teens get real. *U.S. News & World Report* 128 (April 17): 46-55.

Carnegie Council on Adolescent Development. 1992. *A matter of time: Risk and opportunities in the nonschool hours*. New York: Carnegie Corporation.

_____. 1994. *Consultation on afterschool programs*. New York: Carnegie Corporation.

_____. 1995. *Great transitions: Preparing adolescents for a new century*. New York: Carnegie Corporation.

Cart, Michael. 1996. *From romance to realism : Fifty years of growth and change in young adult literature*. New York: HarperCollins.

_____. 1998. Young adult library service redux? *Journal of Youth Services in Libraries* 11 (4): 391-395.

Caywood, Caroline A. 1995. *Youth participation in school and public libraries: It works.* Chicago: Young Adult Library Services Assn.

Chelton, Mary Kay. 1994. *Excellence in library services to young adults: The nation's top programs.* Chicago: American Library Assn.

_____. 1997. *Excellence in library services to young adults: The nation's top programs.* 2nd ed. Chicago: American Library Assn.

_____. 2000. *Excellence in library services to young adults: The nation's top programs.* 3rd ed. Chicago: American Library Assn.

Costello, Joan, Sam Whalen, Julie Spielberger, et al. 2001. Promoting public library partnerships with youth agencies. *Journal of Youth Services in Libraries* 15 (1): 8-15.

Cox, Robin. 2000. Do not let the library be cool. *Voice of Youth Advocates* 23: 240-241.

D'Elia, George, and Eleanor Jo Rodger. 1994. Public library roles and patron use: Why patrons use the library. *Public Libraries* 33 (May/June): 135-144.

_____. 1994. Public opinion about the roles of the public library in the community: The results of a recent Gallup poll. *Public Libraries* 33 (January/February): 23-28.

_____. 1995. The roles of the public library in the community; the results of a Gallup poll of community opinion leaders. *Public Libraries* 34 (March/April): 94-101.

_____. 1996. Customer satisfaction with public libraries. *Public Libraries* 35 (September/October): 292-297.

Doggett, Sandra L., and Paula Kay Montgomery. 2000. *Beyond the book: Technology integration into the secondary school library media curriculum.* Littleton, Colo.: Libraries Unlimited.

Dresang, Eliza T. 1999. *Radical change: Books for youth in a digital age.* New York: H. W. Wilson.

Farkas, Steve. 1997. *Kids these days: What Americans really think about the next generation.* New York: Public Agenda.

Farmer, Lesley S. 2001. Building information literacy through a whole school reform approach. *Knowledge Quest* 29 (January/February): 20-24.

Federal Interagency Forum on Child and Family Statistics. 1999. *America's children: Key national indicators of well being.* Washington, D.C.: Government Printing Office.

Fenwick, Elizabeth, and Tony Smith. 1993. *Adolescence: The survival guide for parents and teenagers.* New York: Dorling-Kindersly.

Fitzgibbons, Shirley A. 2001. School and public library relationships. *Journal of Youth Services in Libraries* 14 (3): 3-7.

Hackman, Mary H., and Paula Kay Montgomery. 1999. *Library information skills and the high school English program.* Littleton, Colo.: Libraries Unlimited.

Hartzell, Gary. 1994. *Building influence for the school library media specialist.* Worthington, Ohio: Linworth.

Henderson, Nan. 1999. Connecting with today's youth. *Education Digest* 64 (5): 14-16.

Herz, Sarah K. 1996. *From Hinton to Hamlet: Building bridges between young adult literature and the classics.* Westport, Conn.: Greenwood.

Hine, Thomas. 1999. *The rise and fall of the American teenager.* New York: Bard/Avon.

Holt, Glen E., and Leslie Edmonds Holt. 1999. What is it worth? *School Library Journal* 45 (June): 47.

Howe, Neil, and William Straus. 1999. *Millennials rising: The next great generation.* New York: Vintage.

Hundley, Kimberly. 2000. The power of teens. *Today's Librarian* 3 (May): 12–16.

Jaffee, Natalie. 1999. *Youth development: Issues, challenges, and directions.* Philadelphia: Public/Private Ventures. Available [Online]: <www.ppv.org/indexfiles/yd-index.html>.

Johnson, Doug. 1997. *The indispensable librarian: Surviving (and thriving) in school media centers.* Worthington, Ohio: Linworth.

Jones, Patrick. 1998. *Connecting young adults and libraries: A How-to-Do-It Manual.* 2nd ed., revised and expanded. New York: Neal-Schuman.

Jones, Patrick, and Joel Shoemaker. 2001. *Do it right: Best practices for serving young adults in school and public libraries.* New York: Neal-Schuman.

Kan, Katharine. 1998. *Sizzling summer reading programs for young adults.* Chicago: American Library Assn.

Kantrowitz, Barbara. 1999. The truth about tweens. *Newsweek* (October 18): 62-71.

Kids count: Writing public library policies that promote use by young people. 1998. New York: Youth Services Section, New York Library Association.

Krashen, Stephen. 1993. *The power of reading: Insights for the research.* Littleton, Colo.: Libraries Unlimited.

Lance, Keith Curry. 1994. The impact of school library media centers on academic achievement. *School Library Media Quarterly* 22 (spring): 167-172.

Larson, Reed W. 2001. How U.S. children and adolescents spend their time: What it does and doesn't tell us about their development. *Current Directions in Psychological Science* 10 (5): 160-164.

_____. Toward a psychology of positive youth development. 2000. *American Psychologist* 55 (January): 170-183.

Leland, John. The secret life of teens. *Newsweek* (May 10, 1999): 44-52.

Lemonick, Michael. 2000. Teens before their time. *Time* 156 (October 30): 66-74.

Long, Sarah Ann. 2000. Libraries can help build sustainable communities. *American Libraries* 31 (June/July): 7.

Machado, Julie, Barbara Lentz, Rachel Wallace, et al. 2000. A survey of best practices in youth services around the country. *Journal of Youth Services in Libraries* 13 (2): 30-35.

MacRae, Cathi Dunn. 2000. "The evidence is in: How youth advocates must meet the millennium. *Voice of Youth Advocates* 22 (6): 377.

_____. 2000. YA radar: Youth experts screen the teen climate at the dawn of 2000. *Voice of Youth Advocates* 22 (6): 384-387.

Males, Mike. 2001. Does "adolescence" mean "abstain from everything"? *Youth Today* 10 (September): 62.

McCook, Kathleen de la Peña, and Rachel Meyer. 2001. Community initiatives for youth development. *Public Libraries* 40 (September/October): 282-288.

Meyers, Elaine. 1999. The coolness factor: Ten libraries listen to youth. *American Libraries* 30 (November): 42-45.

_____. The road to coolness: Youth rock the public library. *American Libraries* 32 (February): 46-49.

Mirchie, Joan, and Bradford Chaney. 2000. *Assessment of the role of school and public libraries in support of education reform.* Washington, D.C.: Westat.

Muller, Patricia. 1999. Come on down! Your leadership role in advancing the national YA agenda. *Journal of Youth Services in Libraries* 12 (2): 13-17.

Mundowney, Joann. 2000. *Hold them in your heart: Successful strategies for library services to at-risk teens.* New York: Neal-Schuman.

Nelson, Lynne. 1999. *Helping youth thrive: How youth organizations can—and do—build developmental assets.* Minneapolis, Minn.: Search Institute.

Nelson, Sandra. 2001. *The new planning for results: A streamlined approach.* Chicago: American Library Assn.

Neuman, Susan B., and Donna Celano. 2001. Access to print in low-income and middle-income communities: An ecological study of four neighborhoods. *Reading Research Quarterly* 36 (1): 8-26.

Pittman, K. J., and M. Wright. 1991. *Bridging the gap: A rationale for enhancing the role of community organizations promoting youth development.* Report prepared for the Task Force on Youth Development and Community Programs by the Carnegie Council on Adolescent Development. Washington, D.C.: Center for Youth Development and Policy Research.

Rankin, Virginia. 1999. *The thoughtful researcher: Teaching the research process to middle school students.* Littleton, Colo.: Libraries Unlimited.

Reinventing adolescent literacy for new times: Perennial and millennial issues. 2000. *Journal of Adolescent and Adult Literacy* (February): 400-420.

Safe passage through adolescence: Communities protecting the health and hopes of youth—lessons learned for W. K. Kellogg Foundation programming. 1998. Battle Creek, Mich.: W. K. Kellogg Foundation.

Scales, Peter. 1998. *Developmental assets: A synthesis of the scientific research on adolescent development.* Minneapolis, Minn.: Search Institute.

_____. 2001. The public image of adolescents. *Society* 38 (May/June): 64-71.

Schneider, Barbara, and David Stevenson. 2001. *The ambitious generation: America's teenagers, motivated but directionless.* New Haven, Conn.: Yale Univ. Pr.

Some things do make a difference for youth: A compendium of evaluations of youth programs and practices. 1997. Washington, D.C.: American Youth Policy Forum.

Spitzer, Kathy, and Michael Eisenberg. 1999. *Information literacy: Essential skills for the Information Age.* Syracuse, N.Y.: ERIC Clearinghouse on Information and Technology.

Standards for public library services to young adults. 1996. Boston: Massachusetts Library Association.

Stanley, Deborah B. 2000. *Practical steps to the research process for middle school.* Littleton, Colo.: Libraries Unlimited.

Starkman, Neil, Peter Scales, and Clay Roberts. 1999. *Great places to learn: How asset building schools help students succeed.* Minneapolis, Minn.: Search Institute.

Stepp, Laura Sessons. 2000. *Our last best shot: Guiding our children through early adolescence.* New York: Riverhead.

Tapscott, Don. 1997. *Growing up digital: The rise of the net generation.* New York: McGraw-Hill.

Teens under pressure, coping well. 1999. *Count on Shell: A publication of Shell Oil Company* 1 (4): 1-7.

Thompson, Helen M., and Susan Henly. 2000. *Fostering information literacy: Connecting national standards, Goals 2000, and the SCANS Report.* Littleton, Colo.: Libraries Unlimited.

U.S. Dept of Commerce. National Telecommunications and Information Administration. 2000. *Closing the digital divide.* Washington, D.C.: Government Printing Office. Available [Online]: <http://digital.divide.gov>.

U.S. Dept. of Health and Human Services. Administration for Children and Families. 1988. *Positive youth development in the United States: Research findings on evaluations of positive youth development programs.* Washington, D.C.: Government Printing Office. Available [Online]: <http:aspe.hhs.gov/hsp/PositiveYouthDev99/index.htm>.

_____. 2000. *Youth who turned their lives around: And the programs that helped them.* Washington, D.C.: Government Printing Office.

Urban Libraries Council. Public libraries as partners in youth development. Available [Online]: <www.urbanlibraries.org/youth.html>.

Volkman, John D. 1998. *Cruising through research: Library skills for young adults.* Littleton, Colo.: Libraries Unlimited.

Walter, Virginia. 1995. *Output measures and more: Planning and evaluating public library services for young adults.* Chicago: American Library Assn.

Wemmet, Lisa. 1997. Librarians as advocates for young adults. *Journal of Youth Services in Libraries* 11 (2): 168-176.

Who are vulnerable youth? 2001. Powerful pathways: Framing options and opportunities for vulnerable youth. Available [Online]: <www.forumforyouthinvestment.org/respapers.htm>. 19 October 2001.

Young adults and public libraries: A handbook of materials and services. 1998. Mary Ann Nichols and C. Allen Nichols, eds. Westport, Conn.: Greenwood.

Youth development: Issues, challenges, and directions. 2000. Philadephia: Public/Private Ventures. Available [Online]: <www.ppv.org/indexfiles/ydindex.html>. 9 January 2002.

Zinn, Laura. 1994. Teens: Here comes the biggest wave yet. *Business Week* (April 14): 79+.

Zollo, Peter. 1999. *Wise up to teens: Insight into marketing and advertising to teenagers.* 2nd ed. Ithaca, N.Y.: New Strategist.

INDEX